A Taste of Enchantment

Treasured Recipes from
The Junior League of Albuquerque

A Taste of Enchantment

Copyright © 2001

The Junior League of Albuquerque

P.O. Box 8858
Albuquerque, New Mexico 87198-8858
505-260-0199   800-753-7731
Fax 505-260-0393   web site: www.jlabq.org

Library of Congress Number: 2001 131264
ISBN: 0-9609278-1-6

Photographer: Peter Vitale

Designed, Edited, and Manufactured by
Favorite Recipes® Press
An imprint of

FRP

P.O. Box 305142
Nashville, Tennessee 37230
1-800-358-0560

Art Director: Steve Newman
Project Manager: Susan Larson

Manufactured in the United States of America
First Printing: 2001   10,000 copies

The inspiring photography for
A Taste of Enchantment
has been graciously donated by
Peter Vitale of Santa Fe and New York.

*When prepared with love and care, good cooking is
not only nourishing to the body, but to the soul as well.*
Peter Vitale

For more of Peter Vitale's work, please refer to:
Southwest Style—A Home-Lover's Guide to Architecture and Design
by Linda Mason Hunter
photography by Peter Vitale

A Toast to Collaboration

Cris Abbott, Chairman
Melinda Browning, Art and Design
Patricia Kalb, Marketing
Heather Hagen-Archer, Recipes

Jennifer Bither
Myra Blottner
Julia Bursum
Amy Campbell
Tommie Carter
Kim Federici
Karen Harmon

Kois Hunnicutt
Marnie Kern
Jennifer Krone
Charlotte Lamont
Judy Loutfy
Karen Lynch
Eleanore Macnish
Jami Pond

Carolyn Pratt
Ginger Rivenbark
Lisa Robinson
Reba Darr Stolp
Ann Travelstead
Tomai Webb
Dana Wilson

Advisors

Jane Armayor   *Lynn Villella*

Nancy Blaugrund
Judy Chreist
Elaine Frassanito

Nancy Herring
Connie Johnson
Marianne Kelly

Sue McWilliams
Kathleen Raskob
Dulcie Schalk

Mission Statement

The Junior League of Albuquerque is an
organization of women committed to promoting voluntarism,
developing the potential of women and improving the community
through the effective action and leadership of trained volunteers.
Its purpose is exclusively educational and charitable.

Table of Contents

Introduction

New Mexico: The Land of Enchantment. For centuries, New Mexico has captivated the hearts of residents and visitors alike. We have a society that is muy simpático, a gentle blending of Native American, Hispano, Anglo, and other cultures that provides a lifestyle unlike any other.

Experiencing New Mexico is a feast for the senses. Landscapes of majestic mountains, expansive sand dunes, and open space as far as the eye can see produce a quality of light that results in turquoise skies by day and opalescent sunsets of vivid reds, pinks, purples, and orange.

Our tastes and attitudes are varied and plentiful; we can be formal with a southwestern flair or casual, yet sophisticated. We are unique in the manner in which we entertain and in the way each cook infuses into her dishes her own personal taste of enchantment.

Our cultures, topography, attitudes, and cuisine are ingredients for a delicious recipe for living. As we gather at our tables, each of these influences is present; none overpowers the other.

Within these pages, you will find treasured recipes for both cooking and living. We offer our highly esteemed traditional fare alongside new and inventive dishes that reflect modern-day southwestern lifestyles. Our favorite restaurants have graciously provided their perennial pleasures to enhance your enchanted journey into New Mexico's cuisine and culture.

Junior League OF ALBUQUERQUE

Is it Chile or Chili?

The Red and the Green of the Issue

New Mexicans share a love story with the spicy and seductive chile pepper. In September of every year, the pungent aroma of chiles roasting on an open fire permeates your nostrils and signals the coming of fall.

Legends are plentiful regarding the introduction of chile into our diets, including accounts from the nineteenth century that said Spanish priests were concerned that chile peppers were aphrodisiacs and warned against eating them. In a wider context, however, chiles have proven themselves as roving ambassadors, with three-quarters of the global population including chiles in their diet on a regular basis. Chiles are the most widely used seasoning in the world; however, more chile is consumed in one day in New Mexico than in the rest of the world put together.

As with any fresh vegetable, green chiles should be shiny, firm, and heavy for their size. Green chile is normally roasted or grilled before using, as the outer skin can give off a bitter flavor and must be removed. Roasting makes it easier to remove the skin and also brings out a richer flavor. Simply place the chiles over an open fire or under your broiler and turn them until their outer skin is heavily blistered. Place in a plastic bag for ten or fifteen minutes and you will find that the skin easily slips away from the pepper. You may use them immediately or freeze them. If freezing, you may put them away peeled or with their blistered skin still adhering—it is simply your personal choice.

Red chiles are simply the ripened form of the green chiles. They are normally dried and ground into an inspiring powder, which is then used in abundance either as a spice to liven up the flavor of a dish, or simply as a basis for a rich, smoky, velvet sauce to mix into soups and stews, as well as robust meat dishes.

Whatever your preference, we urge you to embrace our treasured "jewels of the desert" and open up your palate to an exciting and seductive array of flavors.

Oh, and by the way, chile is the preferred spelling of the pepper and the spice; however chili is also accepted. We've heard that Texans mix meat with our luscious red sauce and call it "chili."

Adobe Aperitivo
Appetizers

The Art of Albuquerque

Albuquerque sits in the beautiful and historic Rio Grande Valley, with its huge sweep of mountains to the east and oceans of desert to the west. Bisecting the state from north to south with grace and beauty, the Rio Grande forms our backbone, its waters giving birth to villages and pueblos that have developed into an abundant society that we enjoy today. From this diverse topography weaves a complex tapestry of soul and form, offering inspiration, anonymity, and a fertile environment from all walks of life.

Everywhere you turn in Albuquerque, you experience the infusion of art into everyday life—from elaborate highway buttresses to the many venues of artistic expression throughout the city. Old Town Plaza, the original colony of Villa de Albuquerque, is centered around the thick, adobe walls of San Felipe de Neri Church, which still stands today. This historic spine of Albuquerque's cultural corridor is further enhanced by the nostalgia of Route 66. These areas and others open their arms to natives and tourists from all over the world.

It is this unique allure—the aura of romance and the rich cultural matrix—that has made New Mexico known around the world as a mecca for creative arts, hands, and minds.

WELLS FARGO BANK NEW MEXICO

Cocktails for a Crowd

Luscious Appetizers for any Season

Señorita's Shrimp and Capers

Sunset Caponata with Grilled Bread

Savory Cheese Straws

Smoked Salmon Cheesecake

Chicken Liver Pâté

Asparagus and Prosciutto Bundles

Triple-Chocolate Biscotti

Serve with plenty of chilled champagne or white wine, pinot noir
and an elegant flavored coffee.

Starters with Finesse

When You Don't Have All Day to Cook

Aztec Artichoke Squares

Mushroom-Stuffed French Bread

Kalamata Tapenade

Mesa Verde Salad

Five-Minute Peach Sherbet

Serve with a peach or mango-flavored iced tea.

Asparagus and Prosciutto Bundles

4 dozen thin fresh asparagus spears
Salt to taste
2¹/2 ounces soft goat cheese, at room temperature
2 tablespoons chopped fresh basil
1 tablespoon pine nuts, toasted, chopped
1 tablespoon water
1 tablespoon grated orange zest
Pepper to taste
2 ounces prosciutto, thinly sliced, cut into
2 dozen 1×4-inch strips

Cut the stalks from the asparagus, leaving 2-inch-long tips; discard the stalks. Combine the asparagus tips and salt with enough water to cover in a saucepan. Bring to a boil. Boil for 1 minute or until tender-crisp; drain. Transfer to paper towels to completely drain.

Combine the goat cheese, basil, pine nuts, water and orange zest in a bowl and mix well. Season with salt and pepper. Spread about 1 teaspoon of the cheese mixture over each prosciutto strip. Arrange 2 asparagus tips at the short end of each strip. Roll to enclose the filling, pressing the seams to seal. Chill, covered, until serving time.

Yield: 2 dozen bundles

*Wild asparagus grows along the riverbanks of New Mexico.
It is delicate but intensely flavorful. Knowing its
whereabouts is a closely held secret that you do not
divulge . . . even to your best friend!*

Aztec Artichoke Squares

1/2 cup chopped onion
1/2 cup water
4 eggs, beaten
1/4 cup fine bread crumbs
1/2 teaspoon salt
1/8 teaspoon pepper
1/8 teaspoon dried oregano, crushed
2 or 3 drops of hot pepper sauce
2 cups shredded Cheddar cheese
2 (6-ounce) jars marinated artichoke hearts, drained,
finely chopped
Pimento strips (optional)

Combine the onion and water in a saucepan. Cook for 5 minutes or until tender; drain. Combine the eggs, bread crumbs, salt, pepper, oregano and hot pepper sauce in a bowl and mix well. Stir in the onion, cheese and artichokes.

Spread the artichoke mixture in a greased 7×11-inch baking pan. Bake at 350 degrees for 17 to 18 minutes or until set and light brown. Cut into 1-inch squares. Serve hot, garnished with pimento strips.

Yield: 6 1/2 dozen squares

Quesadillas are actually a savory appetizer that has evolved over the years. While they did not originate in New Mexico, New Mexicans especially savor them with an extra dollop of BUENO® green chile on top.

Spiced Carrots with Dill

6 medium carrots, peeled   1 tablespoon mustard seeds
1 cup apple cider vinegar   1 tablespoon pickling spice
1 cup water   1/2 teaspoon dillweed
3/4 cup sugar

Cut the carrots into 3-inch-long pieces. Combine the carrots with enough water to cover in a saucepan. Cook for 10 minutes; drain. Let stand until cool. Cut each carrot piece into quarters or eighths, depending upon the diameter of the carrots. The smaller pieces will absorb the dill flavor more readily.

Combine the cider vinegar, water, sugar, mustard seeds, pickling spice and dillweed in a saucepan and mix well. Bring to a simmer, stirring occasionally. Simmer for 10 minutes. Stir in the carrots. Bring to a boil, stirring occasionally. Remove from heat. Let stand until cool. Pour into a 1-quart jar with a tight-fitting lid. Store in the refrigerator for 3 to 4 weeks.

Yield: 1 (1-quart) jar

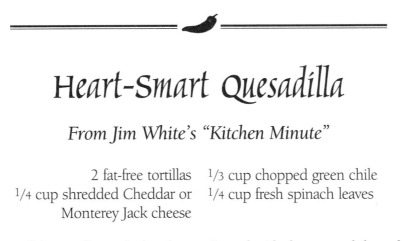

Heart-Smart Quesadilla

From Jim White's "Kitchen Minute"

2 fat-free tortillas   1/3 cup chopped green chile
1/4 cup shredded Cheddar or   1/4 cup fresh spinach leaves
Monterey Jack cheese

Sprinkle 1 of the tortillas with the cheese. Spread with the green chile and sprinkle with the spinach. Top with the remaining tortilla. Arrange the quesadilla on a nonstick baking sheet. Bake at 350 degrees for 10 minutes or until the cheese melts.

Yield: 1 serving

Southwestern Stuffed Mushrooms

3 dozen large mushrooms
4 garlic cloves, minced
1¼ cups (2½ sticks) butter
3 small green onions, chopped
2 to 3 tablespoons BUENO®
frozen green chile

½ cup fine bread crumbs
1½ teaspoons salt
½ teaspoon nutmeg
¼ teaspoon pepper
⅛ teaspoon dry mustard
Grated Parmesan cheese

Remove the stems from the mushroom caps. Chop the stems and set aside. Sauté the garlic in the butter in a skillet for 1 minute. Dip the mushroom caps in the garlic butter until coated and arrange in a single layer on a baking sheet. Reheat the garlic butter in the skillet. Add the green onions and mushroom stems and mix well. Sauté until tender. Stir in the next 6 ingredients. Remove from heat. Mound the bread crumb mixture in the mushroom caps. Sprinkle with the cheese. Bake at 375 degrees for 15 minutes. Remove to a serving platter.

Yield: 3 dozen mushrooms

Poppy Seed Wafers

1 cup flour
½ teaspoon salt
⅓ cup butter
3 to 5 tablespoons ice water

¾ cup shredded Cheddar
cheese
Poppy seeds to taste
1 egg white, lightly beaten

Combine the flour and salt in a bowl and mix well. Cut in the butter until crumbly. Add just enough ice water to moisten the mixture and mix well. Roll the dough ⅛ inch thick on a lightly floured surface. Spread half the dough with half the cheese. Sprinkle with poppy seeds; fold over. Roll 3/16 inch thick. Brush with the egg white. Sprinkle with the remaining cheese and poppy seeds. Cut into 1×2-inch strips. Arrange the strips on an ungreased baking sheet. Bake at 450 degrees for 10 minutes or until light brown.

Yield: 2 dozen wafers

Savory Cheese Straws

1 (17-ounce) package frozen puff pastry, thawed
2 egg whites
1 tablespoon water

2¹/3 cups (about) freshly grated Parmesan cheese
1/2 cup finely minced fresh herbs (chives or dillweed)

Cut each pastry sheet into halves. Chill, covered, in the refrigerator, until needed. Whisk the egg whites and water in a bowl. Remove 1 pastry half from the refrigerator and roll 1/16 inch thick on a hard surface. Brush lightly with the egg wash. Sprinkle with 1/2 cup plus 2 heaping teaspoons of the cheese and 2 tablespoons of the herbs. Press the cheese and herbs lightly into the dough with a rolling pin. Fold the pastry over to enclose the filling, forming a 6×10-inch rectangle. Brush with the egg wash and sprinkle with 1¹/2 teaspoons of the cheese. Cut into 1/2×6-inch strips with a sharp knife. Arrange the strips on a baking sheet lined with baking parchment, pressing the ends down to the parchment. Place the baking sheet in the freezer. Repeat the process with the remaining pastry, egg wash, cheese and herbs. Bake at 400 degrees for 10 minutes or until golden brown. Remove to a wire rack to cool. Store in an airtight container.

Yield: 80 cheese straws

Señorita's Shrimp and Capers

1 or 2 lemons, cut into halves
3 pounds peeled cooked shrimp
1 cup mayonnaise
1 large purple onion, sliced

1/4 cup sour cream
1 (3-ounce) jar capers, rinsed, drained
Dillweed to taste

Squeeze the lemons over the shrimp in a bowl and toss to mix. Mix the remaining ingredients in a bowl. Add to the shrimp and toss to coat. Chill, covered, for 8 to 10 hours, stirring occasionally. Spoon into a serving bowl. Garnish with sprigs of parsley.

Yield: 10 to 12 servings

Focaccia Crust Pizza

Crust

1¹/2 teaspoons dry yeast   2 cups lukewarm water
1¹/2 teaspoons sugar   2¹/2 cups flour
3 tablespoons lukewarm   2¹/2 tablespoons olive oil
water   ¹/2 cup cornmeal
1¹/2 teaspoons salt

Sauce and Assembly

3 tablespoons olive oil   2¹/2 tablespoons
1 cup sliced mushrooms   chopped garlic
1 cup julienned ham   2 tablespoons chopped
1 cup chopped   fresh oregano
plum tomatoes   1 cup shredded mozzarella
¹/4 cup chopped fresh basil   cheese

For the crust, dissolve the yeast and sugar in 3 tablespoons lukewarm water in a bowl. Stir in the salt and 2 cups lukewarm water. Let stand until foamy. Add the flour and olive oil, stirring until a smooth dough forms. Knead until the dough adheres and forms a ball.

Place the dough in an oiled bowl, turning to coat the surface. Let rise, covered, for 1 hour or until doubled in size. Roll into a circle on a lightly floured surface. Fit into a pizza pan or place on a pizza stone sprinkled with the cornmeal.

For the sauce, heat the olive oil in a skillet until hot. Add the mushrooms, ham, tomatoes, basil, garlic and oregano and mix well. Sauté for 10 minutes.

To assemble, spoon the sauce over the prepared layer. Sprinkle with the cheese. Bake at 400 degrees for 20 to 30 minutes or until brown and bubbly.

Yield: 1 large or 2 small pizzas

Mushroom-Stuffed French Bread

1 loaf French bread
12 ounces Swiss cheese, shredded
8 ounces fresh mushrooms, chopped
3 green onions, chopped
1/2 cup (1 stick) butter or margarine
3 garlic cloves, minced
Juice of 1/2 lemon
1 tablespoon sesame seeds

Cut the loaf lengthwise down the center, leaving both ends intact. Cut the loaf diagonally but not through into 12 to 14 slices. Combine the cheese, mushrooms and green onions in a bowl and mix well. Heat the butter in a saucepan until melted. Stir in the garlic and lemon juice.

Stuff the mushroom mixture between the slices. Drizzle with the butter mixture and sprinkle with the sesame seeds. Wrap in foil. Bake at 350 degrees for 30 minutes.

Yield: 12 to 14 servings

New Mexico was admitted to the Union in 1912. Our diverse culture has been heavily influenced by Spanish, Mexican, and Native American heritage, as well as Anglo; thus creating a diverse society which embraces aspects of all our traditions into everyday life.

Wild Mushroom Torte

Crepes

2 cups milk   1 teaspoon olive oil
6 eggs   1 to 1½ cups flour
1 tablespoon butter, melted   Salt and pepper to taste

Mushroom Filling

¼ cup (½ stick) butter   3 cups chopped Champagne
1 large onion, chopped   mushrooms or chanterelles
3 cups chopped portobellos   Salt and pepper to taste
3 cups chopped oyster   Minced garlic to taste
mushrooms   Minced fresh herbs to taste
3 cups chopped shiitake   1 cup heavy cream
mushrooms

For the crepes, whisk the milk, eggs, butter and olive oil in a bowl until blended. Add the flour, salt and pepper and stir until smooth. Heat a 9-inch crepe pan over high heat until hot. Add 2 to 3 tablespoons of the batter, tilting the pan to coat the bottom. Cook until light brown; turn. Cook until brown. Repeat the process with the remaining batter, stacking the cooled crepes between waxed paper.

For the filling, heat the butter in a skillet until melted. Stir in the onion and mushrooms. Cook until the liquid evaporates, stirring frequently. Season with salt, pepper, garlic and herbs. Stir in the heavy cream. Cook until thickened, stirring frequently.

To assemble, place 1 crepe on a baking sheet. Spread with some of the mushroom mixture. Repeat the stacking process with the remaining crepes and mushroom mixture, ending with a crepe. Bake at 350 degrees for 20 minutes. Cut into wedges.

Yield: 8 servings

Tomato and Goat Cheese Tart

1 tablespoon virgin olive oil
1 large onion, thinly sliced
Salt and pepper to taste
1 refrigerator pie pastry
6 ounces goat cheese, crumbled
2 teaspoons coarsely chopped fresh thyme, or
$1/2$ teaspoon dried thyme
3 medium tomatoes, cut into $1/4$-inch slices

Heat the olive oil in a skillet over medium heat. Add the onion. Sauté for 8 to 10 minutes or until golden brown and caramelized. Season with salt and pepper. Remove from heat.

Arrange the pastry on an ungreased baking sheet. Sprinkle the onion to within 1 inch of the edge. Dot with the cheese and sprinkle with the thyme and pepper. Arrange the tomato slices slightly overlapping over the onion. Sprinkle with salt and pepper.

Fold and crimp the edge of the pastry to form a rim. Bake at 450 degrees for 20 minutes or until golden brown. Remove to a wire rack to cool.

Yield: 6 servings

Smoked Salmon Cheesecake

1/4 cup clarified butter
1/2 cup bread crumbs
1/2 cup grated Parmigiano-Reggiano
24 ounces cream cheese, softened
1/3 cup heavy cream
3 egg yolks
1 tablespoon cornstarch
1 cup chopped leek bulbs

3 tablespoons clarified butter
2/3 pound smoked or fresh salmon, bones removed, chopped
8 ounces Gruyère cheese, grated
1/4 cup sliced fresh wild mushrooms
3/4 teaspoon salt
1/2 teaspoon pepper

Brush the bottom and side of a 9-inch terrine with 1/4 cup clarified butter. Combine the bread crumbs and Parmigiano-Reggiano in a bowl and mix well. Reserve a small amount of the crumb mixture to sprinkle over the top of the cheesecake. Sprinkle the remaining crumb mixture over the bottom and side of the prepared terrine.

Beat the cream cheese, heavy cream, egg yolks and cornstarch in a mixing bowl until smooth, scraping the bowl occasionally. Sauté the leeks in 3 tablespoons clarified butter in a skillet until tender but not brown. Stir the leeks, salmon, Gruyère cheese, wild mushrooms, salt and pepper into the cream cheese mixture. Spoon into the prepared terrine. Sprinkle with the reserved crumb mixture.

Place the terrine in a water bath. Bake at 300 degrees for 1 1/2 hours or until set. Turn off the oven. Let stand in the oven with the door ajar for 1 hour. Remove from oven. Let stand for 2 hours or until room temperature. Remove the cheesecake to a platter. Cut into 3/4-inch slices. Serve with shallot butter or curried mayonnaise.

Yield: 12 to 15 servings

Smoked Salmon Cheesecake is versatile enough to serve as an appetizer, luncheon entrée, or on top of a bed of mixed field greens.

Sunset Caponata

2 tablespoons olive oil
1 large red onion, chopped
1 each large yellow and
  green bell pepper,
  cut into 1-inch cubes
1 to 1 1/2 pounds eggplant,
  cut into 1-inch cubes
1 (16-ounce) can stewed tomatoes

3 garlic cloves, chopped
3 tablespoons red wine vinegar
2 tablespoons tomato paste
1 1/2 teaspoons dried basil
3/4 teaspoon salt
1/3 cup kalamata olives,
  cut into halves
1/4 teaspoon liquid red pepper

Heat the olive oil in a heavy saucepan over medium heat. Add the onion and bell peppers and mix well. Cook for 10 minutes, stirring occasionally. Stir in the eggplant, undrained tomatoes, garlic, wine vinegar, tomato paste, basil and salt and mix well. Cook for 10 minutes, stirring frequently. Stir in the olives and red pepper. Cook, partially covered, for 10 minutes longer or just until the vegetables are tender, stirring occasionally. Remove from heat. Let stand until room temperature. Chill, covered, for up to 1 week.

Yield: 12 servings

Asiago Cheese Spread

1 cup mayonnaise
1 cup sour cream
1/2 cup grated asiago cheese
1/4 cup sliced mushrooms

1/4 cup sliced green onions
1/4 cup chopped sun-dried
  tomatoes, reconstituted
2 tablespoons grated asiago cheese

Combine the mayonnaise, sour cream, 1/2 cup cheese, mushrooms and green onions in a bowl and mix well. Stir in the sun-dried tomatoes. Spoon the cheese mixture into a soufflé dish. Sprinkle with 2 tablespoons cheese. Bake at 350 degrees for 15 minutes or until brown and bubbly. Serve with assorted party crackers or toasted pita bread wedges.

Yield: 20 servings

Tailgater Brie

1 (1-pound) round Brie cheese, chilled
8 sun-dried tomatoes, minced
3 tablespoons grated Parmesan or asiago cheese
3 tablespoons minced Italian parsley
3 tablespoons minced fresh basil
3 garlic cloves or shallots, minced
2 tablespoons chopped pine nuts

Remove the rind from the top of the Brie and place the round on a serving platter. Combine the sun-dried tomatoes, Parmesan cheese, parsley, basil, garlic and pine nuts in a bowl and mix well. Spread the sun-dried tomato mixture over the top of the Brie.

Chill for 2 to 3 hours before serving. Serve with assorted party crackers or baguette slices. Serve leftovers over your favorite pasta.

Yield: 10 to 12 servings

Kalamata Tapenade

1 cup pine nuts
1 cup pitted kalamata olives
2 or 3 garlic cloves, crushed
2 1/2 tablespoons capers, rinsed, drained
2 tablespoons lemon juice
1 tablespoon olive oil
1/2 teaspoon dried thyme or basil
Freshly ground pepper to taste

Combine the pine nuts, olives, garlic, capers, lemon juice, olive oil, thyme and pepper in a food processor container. Process until smooth and of a spreading consistency. Serve with assorted party crackers or sliced party bread.

Yield: 4 to 6 servings

Hot Reuben Spread

2 large packages corned beef, chopped, shredded
1 (29-ounce) can sauerkraut, rinsed, drained
1 pound Swiss cheese, shredded
2 cups mayonnaise
1 medium onion, chopped

Mix all the ingredients in a bowl. Spoon the mixture into a 9×13-inch baking pan. Bake at 350 degrees for 30 minutes. Serve hot with party rye or assorted party crackers.

Yield: 12 to 15 servings

Sun-Dried Tomato Mousse

24 ounces cream cheese
1/4 cup sliced or slivered almonds, toasted, ground
3 tablespoons minced sun-dried tomatoes
2 tablespoons fresh lemon juice
1 bunch tarragon, trimmed
1/8 teaspoon crushed garlic
Salt and pepper to taste

Separate the softened cream cheese into sections to fit the feed tube of the food processor. Add the cream cheese through the feed tube, processing constantly until blended. Turn off the food processor. Add the remaining ingredients. Process until blended. Serve at room temperature with assorted party crackers or crostini.

Yield: 20 servings

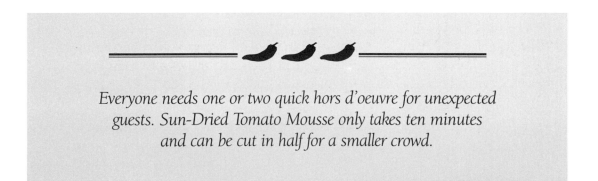

Everyone needs one or two quick hors d'oeuvre for unexpected guests. Sun-Dried Tomato Mousse only takes ten minutes and can be cut in half for a smaller crowd.

Chicken Liver Pâté

From The Albuquerque Petroleum Club

2 pounds bacon, chopped
5 pounds chicken livers
1/4 cup brandy
2 cups cream
2 cups (4 sticks) butter

1 medium onion, chopped
1 cup chopped walnuts
1/2 cup chopped fresh parsley
Salt and pepper to taste

Line a mold with plastic wrap. Fry the bacon in a skillet until crisp. Remove the bacon to a bowl with a slotted spoon, reserving the pan drippings. Cook the livers in the reserved pan drippings until tender, turning frequently. Remove the livers to a bowl with a slotted spoon. Deglaze the hot skillet with the brandy, stirring to loosen any browned bits. Add the cream and mix well. Cook until the mixture is reduced by half, stirring constantly. Process the livers, cream mixture and butter in a food processor until smooth. Pour into a bowl. Stir in the bacon, onion, walnuts, parsley, salt and pepper. Spoon the pâté into the prepared mold; tap the mold on a hard surface several times. Chill, covered, for 8 to 10 hours. Serve with assorted party crackers or toast points.

Yield: 20 to 25 servings

Curried Crab Dip

8 ounces cream cheese
2 cups sour cream
1 cup mayonnaise
1 tablespoon curry powder

2 teaspoons lemon juice
1 1/2 teaspoons salt
1 pound crab meat

Combine the first 6 ingredients in a double boiler. Cook over medium heat until smooth and creamy, stirring frequently. Remove from heat. Stir in the crab meat. Spoon into a chafing dish. Serve with unseasoned crackers or crostini. Use on eggs Benedict instead of hollandaise sauce.

Yield: 10 to 12 servings

Shrimp Dip Magnifico

12 ounces cream cheese, softened
1 cup Thousand Island salad dressing
$^1/_2$ cup mayonnaise
2 pounds large shrimp, cooked, peeled, deveined, chopped
1 cup minced green onions
4 teaspoons Tabasco sauce
1 tablespoon seasoned salt
1 tablespoon prepared horseradish

Beat the cream cheese, salad dressing and mayonnaise in a mixing bowl until blended. Stir in the shrimp, green onions, Tabasco sauce, seasoned salt and horseradish. Chill, covered, for 6 to 8 hours. Serve with assorted party crackers.

Yield: 1 to 1$^1/_4$ quarts

Shrimp and Olive Mousse

6 ounces cream cheese, softened
1 (16-ounce) can pitted black olives, drained, coarsely chopped
4 ounces shrimp, cooked, peeled, deveined, chopped
2 anchovy fillets, chopped (optional)
2 tablespoons lemon juice
1 tablespoon capers, rinsed, drained
1 tablespoon vermouth
1 tablespoon olive oil
1 garlic clove, minced
$^1/_4$ teaspoon thyme

Beat the cream cheese in a mixing bowl until smooth. Stir in the olives, shrimp, anchovies, lemon juice, capers, vermouth, olive oil, garlic and thyme. Serve with assorted party crackers.

Yield: 8 to 10 servings

Very Verde
Salads

The Mystery of the Anasazi

Anasazi is Navajo for "The Ancient Ones." The Anasazi formed communities in the Southwest around 400 A.D., and expanded into thriving pueblos from 800 A.D. to almost 1300 A.D. Representing a broad range of people from various cultures, they developed a complex and vibrant society. Their homes were dramatically situated and finely built, and their lives were rich with artistic quality and material culture. The Anasazi lived in harmony with one another and with nature.

Chaco Canyon was the largest of the Anasazi pueblos. Despite a short growing season and marginal rainfall, it prospered with thirteen separate cities and a population of around five thousand. Chaco Canyon was an economic, political, and religious center for the entire Southwest. Its architecture and masonry were astounding, with buildings up to five stories high. Roads extended to more than fifty different communities, and trade extended as far west as the Pacific Ocean and into southern Mexico.

Around 1300 A.D., Chaco and other Anasazi sites were mysteriously abandoned. While we do not have an explanation, it is believed by many that prolonged drought probably hastened the inhabitants' departure. Few clues were left for our understanding.

Lunch Alfresco

Enjoying the Outdoors and Good Friends

Spiced Carrots with Dill

Ginger Carrot Soup©

Cilantro Chicken Salad

Chocolate Liquid-Center Cake

Cheese Blintz Muffins

Serve with a flavored iced tea or summer spritzer.

Greens 'n' Things

Quick-and-Easy Salad Supper

Raspberry Swirl Peach Soup

Spinach and Goat Cheese Salad

Fruit Salad with Pasta

Marinated Asparagus

Cinnamon Peach Bread

Blend a small amount of peach into softened butter

to complement this menu.

Far East Spinach Salad

Far East Dressing
1 cup vegetable oil
2/3 cup (or less) sugar
1/3 cup ketchup
1/3 cup vinegar
1 small onion, chopped
2 tablespoons Worcestershire sauce
Salt to taste

Salad
1 package fresh spinach, trimmed, torn
1 (14-ounce) can bean sprouts, drained
1 (8-ounce) can water chestnuts, drained, sliced
2 hard-cooked eggs, chopped
5 slices crisp-cooked bacon, crumbled

For the dressing, combine the oil, sugar, ketchup, vinegar, onion, Worcestershire sauce and salt in a jar with a tight-fitting lid. Shake to mix.

For the salad, toss the spinach, bean sprouts, water chestnuts, eggs and bacon in a salad bowl. Add the desired amount of dressing and toss to coat.

Yield: 4 to 6 servings

Festive Romaine Salad

Creamy Poppy Seed Dressing
3/4 cup mayonnaise
1/3 cup sugar
1/4 cup skim milk
2 tablespoons white vinegar
2 tablespoons poppy seeds

Salad
1 head romaine, torn into bite-size pieces, or
mixed salad greens
1 pint fresh strawberries, sliced
1/2 red onion, thinly sliced

For the dressing, whisk the mayonnaise, sugar, skim milk, vinegar and poppy seeds in a bowl until mixed.

For the salad, combine the romaine, strawberries and onion in a salad bowl and mix well. Add the dressing and toss gently to coat. Chill, covered, for 15 minutes before serving.

Yield: 4 servings

Mesa Verde Salad

2 bunches fresh spinach, trimmed,
torn into bite-size pieces
2 Granny Smith apples, thinly sliced
$1/2$ cup chopped walnuts
$1/2$ cup red grapes
$1/2$ cup dried cranberries
1 small log goat cheese, crumbled, or
4 to 6 ounces feta cheese
2 tablespoons olive oil
2 tablespoons apple cider vinegar
Salt and pepper to taste

Toss the spinach, apples, walnuts, grapes, cranberries and goat cheese in a salad bowl. Whisk the olive oil, apple cider vinegar, salt and pepper in a bowl. Drizzle over the salad and toss to coat.

Yield: 8 servings

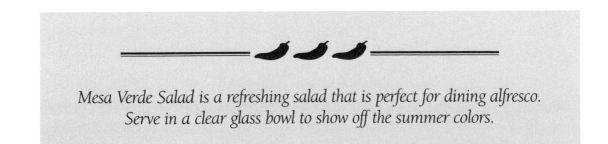

Mesa Verde Salad is a refreshing salad that is perfect for dining alfresco.
Serve in a clear glass bowl to show off the summer colors.

Not Just Salad

10 thin asparagus spears, trimmed
Butter
1 head green leaf lettuce, torn into bite-size pieces
2 cups mixed salad greens
15 cherry tomatoes
1 wedge bleu cheese, chilled, crumbled
$1/2$ cup chopped pecans, toasted
2 tablespoons olive oil
2 tablespoons raspberry vinegar
Salt and pepper to taste

Sauté the asparagus in the butter in a skillet just until tender-crisp; drain. Chill, covered, in the refrigerator.

Toss the leaf lettuce and salad greens in a salad bowl. Top with the asparagus, cherry tomatoes, cheese and pecans. Whisk the olive oil, raspberry vinegar, salt and pepper in a bowl until blended. Drizzle over the salad. Serve immediately.

Yield: 8 servings

Spinach and Goat Cheese Salad

From The Artichoke Café

2 Golden Delicious apples, coarsely chopped
2 tablespoons lemon juice
2 tablespoons honey
2 tablespoons lemon juice
1 tablespoon apple cider vinegar or sherry vinegar
Salt and freshly ground pepper to taste
3 tablespoons extra-virgin olive oil
8 cups baby spinach leaves, trimmed
2/3 cup crumbled goat cheese
1/2 cup walnut halves, toasted

Toss the apples with 2 tablespoons lemon juice in a bowl. Whisk the honey,
2 tablespoons lemon juice, apple cider vinegar, salt and pepper in a bowl. Add the olive
oil gradually, whisking constantly until blended.

Toss the dressing with the apples and spinach in a bowl. Divide the salad evenly
among 4 salad plates. Sprinkle with the cheese and walnuts. Serve immediately.

Yield: 4 servings

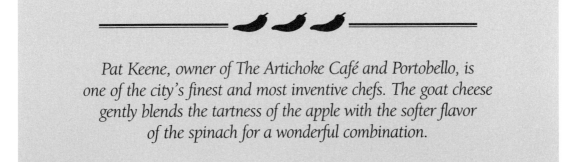

*Pat Keene, owner of The Artichoke Café and Portobello, is
one of the city's finest and most inventive chefs. The goat cheese
gently blends the tartness of the apple with the softer flavor
of the spinach for a wonderful combination.*

Kumquat Winter Salad

Raspberry Vinaigrette

1/4 cup vegetable oil
2 tablespoons sugar
2 tablespoons raspberry vinegar
1/2 teaspoon salt
1/2 teaspoon pepper
1 tablespoon chopped fresh Italian parsley
1/8 teaspoon Tabasco sauce

Salad

1/2 cup slivered almonds
3 tablespoons sugar
2 pomegranates
8 cups mixed gourmet salad greens
1/2 head romaine, torn into bite-size pieces
1 cup kumquat halves
1/2 red onion, thinly sliced, separated into rings

For the vinaigrette, combine the oil, sugar, raspberry vinegar, salt, pepper, parsley and Tabasco sauce in a jar with a tight-fitting lid. Shake to mix. Chill for 3 hours.

For the salad, combine the almonds and sugar in a small skillet. Cook for several minutes or until the sugar dissolves and the almonds are coated, stirring constantly. Let stand until cool.

Remove the seeds from the pomegranates, discarding the flesh. Toss the pomegranate seeds, salad greens, romaine, kumquat halves and onion in a salad bowl. Add the sugared almonds and vinaigrette and toss gently to coat. Serve immediately.

Yield: 8 servings

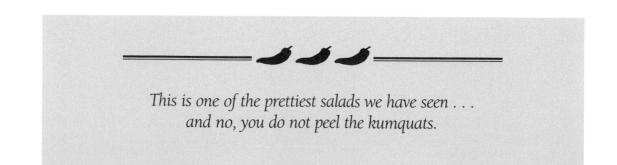

*This is one of the prettiest salads we have seen . . .
and no, you do not peel the kumquats.*

Margarita Coleslaw

Margarita Dressing
3/4 can frozen margarita mix, thawed
1/4 cup vinegar
1/4 cup vegetable oil
1 to 2 tablespoons honey
1 teaspoon celery seeds

Salad
9 cups shredded green cabbage
3 cups shredded red cabbage
2 Granny Smith apples, peeled, chopped
1 cup dried cranberries

For the dressing, combine the margarita mix, vinegar, oil, honey and celery seeds in a jar with a tight-fitting lid. Shake to mix.

For the salad, combine the green cabbage, red cabbage, apples and cranberries in a bowl and mix well. Add the desired amount of dressing and toss to coat. Serve immediately.

Yield: 12 servings

Roasted Pecan Slaw

Creamy Dijon Curry Dressing
1/4 cup sour cream
1/4 cup mayonnaise
1 tablespoon white wine vinegar
1 teaspoon Dijon mustard
1/4 teaspoon curry powder

Salad
1 (10-ounce) package frozen small green peas, thawed, drained
2 cups finely shredded green cabbage
3 green onions, thinly sliced
1 cup dry roasted pecan halves
Salt to taste
6 to 8 romaine leaves

For the dressing, combine the sour cream, mayonnaise, wine vinegar, Dijon mustard and curry powder in a bowl and mix well.

For the salad, combine the peas, cabbage, green onions and 1/2 cup of the pecans in a bowl and mix well. Add the dressing and toss to coat. Season with salt. Spoon the slaw onto a platter lined with the romaine. Sprinkle with the remaining 1/2 cup pecans.

Yield: 6 servings

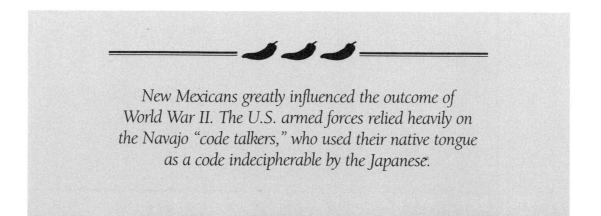

New Mexicans greatly influenced the outcome of World War II. The U.S. armed forces relied heavily on the Navajo "code talkers," who used their native tongue as a code indecipherable by the Japanese.

Napa Slaw with Snow Peas

1 medium cucumber, cut lengthwise into halves,
thinly sliced
1 cup fresh snow peas, cut into halves
1/4 cup rice vinegar
1 tablespoon canola oil
2 teaspoons toasted sesame oil
1/2 teaspoon sugar
1/2 teaspoon salt
1/2 teaspoon red chile paste (optional)
4 cups shredded napa cabbage
1/2 cup honey roasted peanuts,
coarsely chopped (optional)

Toss the cucumber and snow peas in a bowl. Whisk the rice vinegar, canola oil, sesame oil, sugar, salt and red chile paste in a bowl. Pour over the cucumber mixture and toss to coat.

Chill, covered, for 4 to 24 hours, stirring occasionally. Stir in the cabbage and peanuts just before serving.

Yield: 8 servings

Orange Almond Salad

1/4 cup salad oil
2 tablespoons sugar
2 tablespoons malt vinegar
1/4 teaspoon salt
1/8 teaspoon almond extract
6 cups torn mixed greens
Sections of 3 medium oranges, cut into halves
1 cup thinly sliced celery
3 tablespoons sliced green onions
1/3 cup slivered almonds, toasted

Combine the salad oil, sugar, malt vinegar, salt and almond extract in a jar with a tight-fitting lid. Shake until the sugar and salt dissolves. Chill in the refrigerator.

Toss the mixed greens, oranges, celery and green onions in a salad bowl. Sprinkle with the almonds. Add the chilled dressing and toss gently to coat. Serve immediately.

Yield: 6 to 8 servings

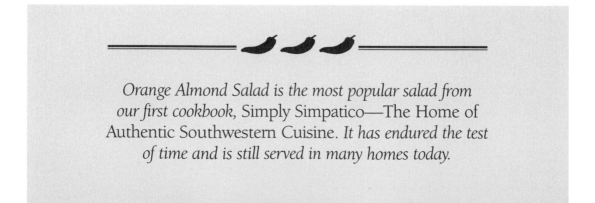

Orange Almond Salad is the most popular salad from our first cookbook, Simply Simpatico—The Home of Authentic Southwestern Cuisine. *It has endured the test of time and is still served in many homes today.*

Jicama Salad with Oranges

2 cups julienned peeled jicama
1¹/2 cups orange sections
1/4 cup julienned red bell pepper
1/4 cup julienned yellow bell pepper
3 tablespoons chopped fresh cilantro
2 teaspoons grated orange zest
2 tablespoons orange juice
Juice of 1 lime
1/4 teaspoon salt
1/8 teaspoon pepper

Combine the jicama, orange sections, bell peppers, cilantro and orange zest in a bowl and mix gently. Whisk the orange juice, lime juice, salt and pepper in a bowl. Pour over the salad and toss gently to coat.

Yield: 2 servings

Pear and Goat Cheese Salad

Pear Vinaigrette

1 tablespoon pear or white wine vinegar	1/2 teaspoon ground white pepper
1 tablespoon walnut oil	1/8 teaspoon kosher salt
1 teaspoon honey	1/3 cup canola oil

Salad

3 cups water	Raw sugar to taste
4 fresh pears, peeled, cored	10 cups spring field greens
12 ounces goat cheese or chèvre	2 ounces dried pears, julienned
3 ounces pine nuts, shelled, chopped	

For the vinaigrette, combine the pear vinegar, walnut oil, honey, white pepper and kosher salt in a blender container. Process until blended. Add the canola oil in a fine stream, processing constantly until smooth. Process for 30 seconds longer.

For the salad, bring the water to a boil in a saucepan over high heat. Add the fresh pears; reduce the heat to simmer. Poach for 4 to 5 minutes; drain. Let stand until cool.

Cut the goat cheese into eight 1 1/2-ounce rounds. Roll each round in the pine nuts and arrange in a single layer in a round 9-inch baking dish. Bake at 400 degrees for 5 minutes or just until the cheese begins to melt.

Cut the pears lengthwise into halves. Cut each half into thin wedges cutting to but not through the bottom and fan on a baking sheet. Sprinkle with raw sugar. Broil for 1 to 2 minutes.

Toss the salad greens and dried pears in a bowl. Add the vinaigrette and toss to coat. Divide the salad equally among 8 salad plates. Top each salad with 1 pear half and 1 goat cheese round.

Yield: 8 servings

Fruit Salad with Pasta

2 cups medium pasta shells
Sections of 2 large oranges
1 unpeeled apple
2 large bananas
1 (20-ounce) can unsweetened pineapple chunks, drained
1 cup red grape halves
1 cup green grape halves
1 cup plain yogurt
1/4 cup frozen orange juice concentrate

Cook the pasta using package directions; drain. Rinse with cool water and drain. Cut the orange sections into halves. Chop the apple into desired size pieces. Cut the bananas into thin slices.

Combine the pasta, orange halves, chopped apple, banana slices, pineapple chunks and grape halves in a large salad bowl and mix gently. Combine the yogurt and orange juice in a bowl and mix well. Add to the pasta mixture and toss to coat. Chill, covered, for several hours before serving.

Yield: 12 servings

Warm Sherried Fruit Salad

1 (16-ounce) can peach halves, drained
1 (16-ounce) can pear halves, drained
1 (15-ounce) can sliced pineapple, drained, cut into halves
1 (8-ounce) jar spiced apple rings, drained, cut into halves
$1/3$ to $1/2$ cup butter or margarine
$1/2$ cup packed light brown sugar
2 tablespoons flour
$3/4$ to 1 cup sherry

Layer the peaches, pears, pineapple and spiced apples in a 2-quart baking dish. Heat the butter in a saucepan over low heat until melted. Stir in the brown sugar and flour. Cook for 1 minute or until smooth, stirring constantly. Add the sherry gradually, stirring constantly.

Cook over medium heat until thickened, stirring constantly. Pour over the prepared layers. Chill, covered, for 8 to 10 hours. Let stand until room temperature. Bake at 350 degrees for 25 minutes or until bubbly. You may add or substitute any canned fruit.

Yield: 10 servings

Marinated Asparagus

2 pounds fresh asparagus spears
1 cup Italian salad dressing
2 hard-cooked eggs, chopped
1/4 cup chopped dill pickles
1/4 cup minced green bell pepper
2 tablespoons chopped fresh parsley
2 tablespoons capers, rinsed, drained

Snap off the thick woody ends of the asparagus. Combine the asparagus with enough water to cover in a saucepan. Bring to a boil. Boil for 6 minutes; drain. Plunge the asparagus into a bowl of ice water to stop the cooking process; drain. Arrange the asparagus in a shallow dish.

Combine the salad dressing, eggs, dill pickles, bell pepper, parsley and capers in a bowl and mix well. Pour over the asparagus, turning to coat. Marinate, covered, in the refrigerator for 3 to 4 hours, turning occasionally. Drain, reserving the marinade. Arrange the asparagus on a serving platter lined with red or green leaf lettuce. Top with the reserved marinade.

Yield: 6 to 8 servings

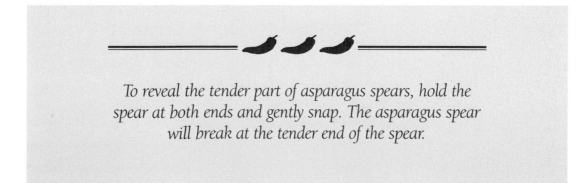

To reveal the tender part of asparagus spears, hold the spear at both ends and gently snap. The asparagus spear will break at the tender end of the spear.

Wild Mushroom Salad with Garlic

From Terra American Bistro

1 cup buttermilk	1 cup polenta
1 cup sour cream	1/2 cup flour
1 cup mayonnaise	1/2 cup cornstarch
2 tablespoons ground pepper	4 cups mixed wild
1 teaspoon ground coriander	mushrooms (shiitake,
Salt to taste	cremini, oyster or chanterelle)
1 1/2 cups olive oil	2 large heads romaine,
1 cup whole peeled garlic	trimmed, separated
cloves, ends trimmed	4 large tomatoes, coarsely
3 cups milk	chopped
2 teaspoons salt	1 cup crumbled bleu cheese

Combine the buttermilk, sour cream, mayonnaise, pepper, coriander and salt to taste in a bowl and mix until blended. Chill, covered, in the refrigerator. Combine the olive oil and garlic in a small ovenproof pan and mix well. Roast, covered, at 250 degrees for 2 1/2 to 3 hours or until the garlic is tender. Remove the cover. Let stand until cool. Strain the garlic oil into a bowl, reserving the garlic cloves. Store the garlic in the refrigerator.

Combine the milk and 2 teaspoons salt in a saucepan. Bring to a simmer over medium heat. Whisk in the polenta gradually. Reduce the heat to low. Cook until the polenta pulls from the side of the saucepan, stirring constantly. Spread the polenta 1/2 inch thick in a shallow rectangular dish. Let stand until cool.

Cut the polenta into cubes. Combine the flour and cornstarch in a bowl and mix well. Add the polenta to the flour mixture and toss to coat. Heat 1 cup of the reserved garlic oil in a large sauté pan or wok over medium-high heat for 2 to 3 minutes. Shake the excess flour from the polenta and add the cubes to the hot garlic oil. Fry for 3 minutes or until the edges of the cubes are brown. Remove the croutons with a slotted spoon to a paper towel to drain, reserving the garlic oil. Add the mushrooms to the reserved garlic oil. Cook until they lose their volume, stirring frequently. Remove the mushrooms with a slotted spoon to a paper towel to drain.

To assemble, cut the lettuce leaves lengthwise into four portions. Toss with the dressing in a large bowl until coated. Top with the warm mushrooms, polenta croutons, reserved garlic, tomatoes and bleu cheese. Serve immediately.

Yield: 6 servings

Warm Potato Salad

6 medium unpeeled potatoes
6 slices bacon, chopped
3/4 cup sliced onion
3 tablespoons sugar
2 tablespoons flour
$1^1/2$ teaspoons salt
1/2 teaspoon celery seeds
1/8 teaspoon pepper
3/4 cup water
1/4 cup vinegar

Combine the potatoes with enough water to cover in a saucepan. Bring to a boil. Boil until tender; drain. Cool slightly. Slice the potatoes into a bowl.

Sauté the bacon and onion in a skillet until the onion is tender and the bacon is cooked through. Stir in the sugar, flour, salt, celery seeds and pepper. Add 3/4 cup water and vinegar and mix well. Bring to a boil.

Boil for 2 minutes, stirring frequently. Pour over the potatoes and toss gently. The flavor of the salad is enhanced if prepared 1 day in advance and stored, covered, in the refrigerator. Reheat before serving.

Yield: 8 servings

Wild Mushroom Salad with Garlic is an ideal year-round salad. The subtle flavor of the roasted garlic blends well with the earthy mushrooms, crispy croutons, and velvet-like dressing. The smell of the roasting garlic will fill your entire house so those who do not love garlic may choose to either omit it or tell others to evacuate.

Sandia Potato Salad

2 pounds new potatoes, cut into quarters
1 cup chopped peeled jicama
$1/2$ cup sliced black olives
$1/4$ cup sliced green olives
2 jalapeño chiles, finely chopped
2 tablespoons snipped fresh parsley
1 tablespoon snipped fresh cilantro
$1/2$ teaspoon salt
$1/2$ teaspoon pepper
1 (8-ounce) bottle ranch salad dressing
Leaf lettuce
18 cherry tomatoes, cut into halves
1 large avocado, sliced
Lime juice

Combine the new potatoes with enough water to cover in a saucepan. Bring to a boil. Boil for 10 minutes; drain.

Combine the new potatoes, jicama, black olives, green olives, jalapeño chiles, parsley, cilantro, salt and pepper in a bowl and mix gently. Add the salad dressing and toss to coat. Chill, covered, for 6 to 24 hours.

Line a salad bowl with leaf lettuce. Add the cherry tomato halves to the potato salad and mix gently. Spoon into the prepared bowl. Brush the avocado slices with lime juice and arrange over the top of the salad. Serve immediately.

Yield: 8 to 10 servings

Casa Grande Salad

$1/2$ cup mayonnaise
$1/4$ cup minced green onions
2 tablespoons BUENO® red chile sauce
2 teaspoons cider vinegar
1 teaspoon onion salt
$1/2$ teaspoon BUENO® chile powder
4 drops of hot pepper sauce
1 (12-ounce) can whole kernel corn, drained
1 (8-ounce) can red kidney beans, drained
1 (7-ounce) can pitted black olives, drained
2 cups shredded lettuce

Combine the mayonnaise, green onions, chile sauce, vinegar, onion salt, chile powder and hot pepper sauce in a bowl and mix well. Chill, covered, in the refrigerator.

Combine the corn, kidney beans and olives in a bowl and mix well. Add the chilled mayonnaise mixture and toss gently to coat. Line a bowl with the lettuce. Spoon the salad over the lettuce.

Yield: 6 to 8 servings

Water Chestnut Salad

1 (17-ounce) can small green peas, drained
1 (16-ounce) can bean sprouts, drained
2 (5-ounce) cans water chestnuts, drained
1 (6-ounce) can mushrooms, drained
1 (4-ounce) jar pimentos, drained, chopped
1 large green bell pepper, chopped
1 large onion, chopped
1 cup chopped celery
1 cup vegetable oil
1 cup sugar
1 cup apple cider vinegar
Salt and pepper to taste

Combine the peas, bean sprouts, water chestnuts, mushrooms, pimentos, bell pepper, onion and celery in a bowl and mix well. Whisk the oil, sugar, cider vinegar, salt and pepper in a bowl. Pour over the vegetables and toss to coat. Chill, covered, for 8 to 10 hours.

Yield: 4 servings

Mexican Chef Salad

Avocado Dressing

1 large avocado, chopped
1/2 cup sour cream
2 tablespoons Italian
   salad dressing
1/2 teaspoon salt
1/8 teaspoon pepper
3/4 teaspoon BUENO®
   chile powder
2 teaspoons minced
   green onions

Salad

4 boneless skinless chicken
   breasts, cooked, sliced
1 head leaf lettuce, torn into
   bite-size pieces
1 (6-ounce) can pitted black
   olives, drained, sliced
1 (16-ounce) can kidney beans,
   rinsed, drained
2 tomatoes, chopped, drained
1 tablespoon BUENO® green
   chile sauce
1/2 cup shredded Cheddar
   cheese
1/2 cup coarsely crushed
   tortilla chips

For the dressing, combine the avocado, sour cream and salad dressing in a bowl and mix until blended. Stir in the salt, pepper, chile powder and green onions. Chill, covered, in the refrigerator.

For the salad, toss the chicken, lettuce, olives, beans, tomatoes and green chile sauce in a bowl. Chill, covered, in the refrigerator. Add the dressing and toss to coat. Sprinkle with the cheese and chips. Serve immediately. To reduce those fat grams, toss the salad with a mixture of the following ingredients: 2 cups nonfat sour cream, 3/4 cup salsa and 1 cup BUENO® frozen green chile.

Yield: 6 servings

Southwestern Cobb Salad

^{3}/4 cup ranch salad dressing
^{3}/4 cup BUENO® salsa
2 ears corn, cooked
1 head Bibb or leaf lettuce, torn
8 to 10 slices crisp-cooked bacon, crumbled
3 cups (^{3}/4-inch-cubes) cooked chicken
^{1}/2 cup crumbled bleu cheese
3 medium tomatoes, chopped
1^1/2 cups drained cooked black beans
2 avocados, cut into ^{3}/4-inch chunks
3 BUENO® corn tortillas, cut into strips, toasted

Combine the salad dressing and salsa in a bowl and mix well. Remove the kernels of corn from the cob with a sharp knife into a bowl. Line a large serving platter with the lettuce.

Layer the crumbled bacon, chicken, bleu cheese, corn kernels, tomatoes, black beans and avocados on the prepared platter. Drizzle with the salad dressing mixture. Arrange the tortilla strips over the top.

Yield: 6 to 8 servings

Antipasto Salad

Balsamic Vinaigrette

1/2 cup olive oil
1/3 cup red wine vinegar
2 tablespoons balsamic vinegar
1 tablespoon water

1 tablespoon Dijon mustard
2 garlic cloves, minced
1/2 teaspoon red pepper flakes

Salad

16 ounces pasta (penne, farfale, etc.)
1 (16-ounce) can garbanzo beans, drained, rinsed
1 (14-ounce) can artichoke hearts, drained, cut into quarters
1 (12-ounce) jar roasted red peppers, drained, rinsed, julienned

1 1/2 cups smoked Gouda or mozzarella cheese cubes
1 (7-ounce) jar oil-pack sun-dried tomatoes, drained, rinsed, julienned
1 (4-ounce) can sliced black olives, drained
10 to 20 pepperoncini
1 cup chopped fresh parsley

For the vinaigrette, combine the olive oil, wine vinegar, balsamic vinegar, water, Dijon mustard, garlic and red pepper flakes in a jar with a tight-fitting lid. Shake to mix.

For the salad, cook the pasta using package directions until al dente; drain. Cool slightly. Combine the pasta, beans, artichokes, roasted red peppers, cheese, sun-dried tomatoes, olives, pepperoncini and parsley in a bowl and mix gently. Add the vinaigrette and toss to coat.

Yield: 8 servings

Couscous Salad with Feta Cheese

1 cup water
2/3 cup couscous
3/4 cup drained canned chick-peas
3/4 cup crumbled feta cheese
1/3 cup pitted kalamata olives
1/3 cup chopped red onion
1/4 cup chopped yellow bell pepper
1/4 cup chopped red bell pepper
3 tablespoons minced fresh mint
3 tablespoons olive oil
3 tablespoons fresh lemon juice

Bring the water to a boil in a saucepan. Stir in the couscous. Cook using package directions. Let stand until cool. Fluff with a fork.

Combine the couscous, chick-peas, feta cheese, olives, onion, bell peppers, mint, olive oil and lemon juice in a bowl and mix well. Chill, covered, until serving time.

Yield: 4 to 6 servings

Each August, Santa Fe is host to Indian Market. Clearly the most prestigious Native American art exhibition in the country, over six hundred booths house the compelling creations of twelve hundred artists from over a hundred tribes and pueblos. This annual event draws large numbers of visitors from all over the world to New Mexico. Artists' entries are screened for authenticity and quality.

Hearty Corn Bread Salad

1 (8-ounce) package corn bread mix
1/3 cup milk
1 egg
4 medium tomatoes, peeled, chopped
1 green bell pepper, chopped
1/2 small onion, chopped
1/2 cup chopped sweet pickles
8 slices crisp-cooked bacon, crumbled
1 cup mayonnaise
1/4 cup sweet pickle juice

Combine the corn bread mix, milk and egg in a bowl and mix well. Spoon the batter into a greased 8×8-inch baking pan. Bake at 400 degrees for 20 minutes. Let stand until cool; crumble.

Toss the tomatoes, bell pepper, onion, pickles and bacon gently in a bowl. Combine the mayonnaise and sweet pickle juice in a bowl and mix well. Layer the corn bread, tomato mixture and mayonnaise mixture 1/2 at a time in a large glass bowl. Chill, covered, for 2 hours.

Yield: 8 servings

Spring Vegetable and Chicken Salad

Lemon Cream Dressing

1/4 cup lemon juice 2 tablespoons chopped
3/4 teaspoon sugar fresh dillweed
3/4 teaspoon salt 1 tablespoon each chopped
1/3 teaspoon white pepper fresh basil and chives
1 cup heavy cream, chilled

Spring Vegetables and Chicken

4 cups chicken broth 1 pound boneless skinless
4 medium carrots chicken breasts
2 dozen asparagus spears

Salad

2 medium cucumbers 2 shallots, finely minced
2 red bell peppers 6 cups mixed field greens

For the dressing, whisk the lemon juice, sugar, salt and white pepper in a bowl. Add the heavy cream gradually, whisking constantly until the dressing is thick but still fluid. Stir in the dillweed, basil and chives. Chill, covered, in the refrigerator.

For the vegetables, bring the broth to a boil in a saucepan over medium-high heat. Cut the carrots into 1/2-inch slices. Trim the asparagus. Add the carrots and asparagus to the saucepan; reduce heat. Simmer for 3 minutes or until the vegetables are tender-crisp. Remove the vegetables to a bowl with a slotted spoon, reserving the broth. Let stand until cool. Chill, covered, in the refrigerator. Combine the chicken with the reserved broth in the saucepan. Simmer, covered, for 7 to 10 minutes or until the chicken is cooked through, turning occasionally; drain. Cool slightly. Chill, covered, in the refrigerator.

For the salad, cut the tips from the asparagus spears and set the tips aside. Coarsely chop the asparagus stalks and carrots and place in a bowl. Peel, seed and coarsely chop the cucumbers. Chop the bell peppers coarsely. Chop the chicken into bite-size pieces. Add the cucumbers, bell peppers, shallots and chicken to the asparagus mixture. Add the dressing and toss gently to coat. Arrange the field greens on each of 4 plates. Mound the chicken salad on top of the greens. Top with the reserved asparagus tips.

Yield: 4 servings

Cilantro Chicken Salad

Sesame Dressing

2 bunches green onions, minced
1/4 cup sesame oil
1/4 cup white vinegar
2 to 3 tablespoons sugar

2 tablespoons soy sauce
1 teaspoon crushed red pepper
2 garlic cloves, minced

Salad

1/4 cup soy sauce
4 teaspoons sugar
1 tablespoon sherry
2 teaspoons hoisin sauce
1 garlic clove, crushed
3 boneless skinless chicken breasts
2 egg yolks, beaten
5 tablespoons sesame seeds
1 cup rice flour
1 cup peanut oil

1/2 head iceberg lettuce, finely shredded
1/4 head red cabbage, finely shredded
1/2 (6-ounce) package chow mein noodles
1/4 cup cashews, almonds or peanuts
1 bunch cilantro, stemmed
1 tablespoon sesame seeds, toasted

For the dressing, combine the green onions, sesame oil, vinegar, sugar, soy sauce, red pepper and garlic in a jar with a tight-fitting lid. Shake to mix.

For the salad, whisk the soy sauce, sugar, sherry, hoisin sauce and garlic in a bowl. Pour over the chicken in a shallow dish, turning to coat. Marinate, covered, in the refrigerator for 1 to 2 hours, turning occasionally; drain. Dip the chicken in the egg yolks. Coat with 5 tablespoons sesame seeds and then with the rice flour.

Heat the peanut oil in a skillet until hot. Add the chicken. Fry until cooked through and brown and crisp on both sides; drain. Let stand until cool. Chill until serving time.

Cut the chicken into strips. Toss with the lettuce and cabbage in a salad bowl. Add the noodles, cashews, cilantro and 1 tablespoon toasted sesame seeds. Add the dressing and toss to coat. Serve immediately.

Yield: 4 or 5 servings

Tinnie's Thai Chicken Salad

From Tinnie Mercantile Store & Deli

Peanut Dressing

1 cup soy sauce	1/2 cup sesame oil
1/2 cup creamy peanut butter	2 tablespoons sugar
1/2 cup rice vinegar	1 tablespoon hot chile oil

Salad

2 pounds linguini	4 bunches green onions, sliced
1/4 cup sesame oil	
1 1/4 pounds snow peas, trimmed, sliced	2 bunches cilantro, trimmed, chopped
Salt to taste	4 jalapeño chiles, minced
2 roasted chickens, boned, shredded	Napa cabbage leaves
	Pine nuts

For the dressing, combine the soy sauce, peanut butter, rice vinegar, sesame oil, sugar and hot chile oil in a blender or food processor container. Process until smooth.

For the salad, cook the pasta using package directions. Rinse with cold water; drain. Toss the pasta with the sesame oil in a bowl. Cook the snow peas in boiling salted water in a saucepan for 1 minute or until crisp. Drain and rinse with cool water. Add the snow peas, chicken, green onions, cilantro and jalapeño chiles to the pasta and toss to mix. Add the dressing and mix well. Chill, covered, in the refrigerator. Mound the salad on a large serving platter lined with cabbage leaves. Sprinkle with pine nuts. Serve immediately.

Yield: 20 servings

Wild Rice Chicken Salad

2 cups water
2/3 cup wild rice, rinsed
2/3 cup mayonnaise
1/3 cup milk
1/3 cup lemon juice
1/2 small onion, minced
2 1/2 cups chopped cooked chicken breasts
1 (8-ounce) can water chestnuts, drained, sliced
Salt and pepper to taste
2 cups green grape halves
1 cup cashews

Bring the water to a boil in a saucepan. Stir in the wild rice. Cook, covered, over low heat for 45 minutes or until tender. Let stand until cool.

Combine the mayonnaise, milk, lemon juice and minced onion in a bowl and mix well. Stir in the chopped chicken, water chestnuts and cooled wild rice. Chill, covered, for 2 to 3 hours. Season with salt and pepper. Fold in the grapes and cashews just before serving.

Yield: 6 servings

Roquefort Dressing

1 cup reduced-fat cottage cheese
1/2 cup buttermilk
2 tablespoons wine vinegar
2 ounces Roquefort or bleu cheese, crumbled
Salt and freshly ground pepper to taste

Combine the cottage cheese, buttermilk and wine vinegar in a blender container. Process until blended. Add half the Roquefort cheese and process until smooth. Stir in the remaining cheese, salt and pepper. Store, covered, in the refrigerator until serving time.

Yield: 1 1/2 cups

Swiss Salad Sauce

1/4 cup mayonnaise
3 tablespoons milk or cream
2 tablespoons vegetable oil
2 tablespoons vinegar
2 tablespoons soy sauce
1 teaspoon prepared mustard
1 garlic clove, crushed

Combine the mayonnaise, milk, oil, vinegar, soy sauce, prepared mustard and garlic in a bowl and mix well. Store, covered, in the refrigerator until serving time. Serve over your favorite mixed greens.

Yield: 1 cup

Minted Orange Salad Dressing

3 tablespoons orange juice
2 tablespoons honey
1 tablespoon lemon juice
1 tablespoon minced fresh mint
1 cup plain yogurt

Whisk the orange juice, honey, lemon juice and mint in a bowl. Whisk in the yogurt. Chill, covered, until serving time. Toss with orange sections and seedless grapes, or your favorite fresh fruit combination.

Yield: 1 1/3 cups

Raspberry Piñon Vinaigrette

From Jim White's "Kitchen Minute"

2 cups extra-virgin olive oil
1 cup balsamic vinegar
1 cup piñons, toasted, finely chopped
1 (8-ounce) jar raspberry preserves
1/4 cup Worcestershire sauce
1/4 cup kosher salt
3 tablespoons Tabasco sauce
2 tablespoons Italian seasoning
2 tablespoons granulated garlic
2 tablespoons cracked pepper

Combine the olive oil, balsamic vinegar, piñons, preserves, Worcestershire sauce, kosher salt, Tabasco sauce, Italian seasoning, garlic and cracked pepper in a jar with a tight-fitting lid. Shake to mix.

Yield: 4 cups

Fireside Fiestas
Soups and Stews

Spiritual Harmony

The name "Taos" comes from the Tiwa word for "red willow place." Legend holds that an eagle first led the ancestors of the Taos Indians to the area some eight hundred years ago. Descendants of the Anasazi gazed upon the majestic landscape with its rich soil and plentiful water and chose it for their permanent home.

In 1898, two artists from the East, Ernest Blumenschein and Bert Phillips, were on a sketching trip when their wagon wheel broke and stranded them in Taos. Overwhelmed by its magnificent light and exotic terrain, Blumenschein continued to visit Taos each summer for many years, and eventually moved there in 1919.

From this artistic embryo came the six original members of the Taos Society of Artists, a primary force in establishing Taos as a significant center for art and fine crafts. Today, this quaint little town has more artists per capita than Paris and more nonprofit cultural institutions than cities many times its size.

The city is celebrated widely for the way it changes people's lives. It overwhelms them with a pleasing and uncontrollable urge to quit their jobs, pack their belongings, and relocate to Taos.

Dardanes & Co.

PRINTING • DESIGN • ADVERTISING

Photo taken at the Clay Angel
Santa Fe, New Mexico

Field Goal Football Party

Make a Casual Event Special

Heart-Smart Quesadillas

Mesa Verde Salad

Male Chauvinist Chili

Jalapeño Corn Bread

Gila Monster Cookies

Green Chile Apple Cobbler

An assortment of imported beers gives this menu an added flair.

Liquid Gold

A Soup Buffet for the Hurried Cook

Corn and Wild Rice Soup

Mushroom Soup with Brie

Portobello Barley Soup

Blanco Chili

Serve with warm flour tortillas and French bread.

Raspberry Swirl Peach Soup

1 (48-ounce) can peaches in light syrup
3 cups peach nectar
$1/2$ cup sugar
1 cup fresh or frozen raspberries
$1/4$ cup sugar
1 tablespoon nutmeg
Sprigs of fresh mint

Combine the undrained peaches, nectar and $1/2$ cup sugar in a food processor container. Process until smooth. Chill, covered, in the refrigerator.

Process the raspberries and $1/4$ cup sugar in a food processor until puréed. Chill, covered, in the refrigerator.

Ladle the peach mixture into chilled soup bowls. Swirl 2 to 3 tablespoons of the raspberry purée over the top of each serving. Sprinkle with the nutmeg. Top with sprigs of mint.

Yield: 6 servings

For an unusual winter warmer, serve Raspberry Swirl Peach Soup hot. Add $1/2$ teaspoon cinnamon to the soup.

Cream of Avocado Soup

1 (14-ounce) can chicken broth
2 medium avocados, chopped
2 tablespoons dry sherry
3/4 teaspoon salt
1/2 teaspoon onion powder
1/2 teaspoon dillweed
1 cup half-and-half
3 or 4 avocado slices

Combine the broth, 2 avocados, sherry, salt, onion powder and dillweed in a blender container. Process until smooth. Stir in the half-and-half. Chill, covered, until serving time. Ladle into chilled soup bowls. Top each serving with a slice of avocado.

Yield: 3 or 4 servings

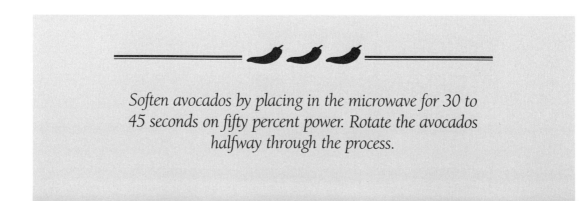

Soften avocados by placing in the microwave for 30 to 45 seconds on fifty percent power. Rotate the avocados halfway through the process.

Black Bean Soup

From Jane Butel

3 cups dried black beans
5 cups chicken broth
4 to 5 cups water
1 cup chopped onion
2 meaty ham hocks
5 garlic cloves, minced
2 tablespoons ground hot chile
1 tablespoon cumin
$2^{1}/_{2}$ teaspoons salt
$^{1}/_{4}$ cup pickled jalapeño chile juice, or to taste
Sour cream
Minced green onions
Crushed caribe chiles
6 to 8 tablespoons sherry or rum

Sort and rinse the beans. Combine the beans, broth, water, onion, ham hocks, garlic, hot chile, cumin and salt in a stockpot. Bring to a boil; reduce the heat. Simmer until the beans are tender, adding additional water as needed. Stir in the jalapeño chile juice. Adjust the seasonings. Spoon the soup into soup bowls. Top each serving with a dollop of sour cream and sprinkle with green onions and caribe chiles. Drizzle each serving with 1 tablespoon sherry.

Yield: 6 to 8 servings

Corn and Wild Rice Soup

12$1/2$ cups reduced-sodium chicken broth
1$1/4$ cups wild rice
6$1/4$ cups corn kernels
2 tablespoons vegetable oil
10 ounces kielbasa, chopped
2 medium onions, chopped
3 carrots, chopped
1$1/2$ cups half-and-half
Salt and pepper to taste
Chives and parsley

Bring 5 cups of the broth to a boil in a saucepan. Stir in the wild rice. Simmer, covered, for 40 minutes or until the rice is tender. Process 3$3/4$ cups of the corn and 1$1/2$ cups of the broth in a food processor until puréed.

Heat the oil in a large saucepan until hot. Sauté the sausage, onions and carrots in the hot oil for 3 minutes or until brown. Add the remaining 6 cups broth and mix well. Simmer for 15 minutes or until the carrots are tender, stirring occasionally. Stir in the rice, corn purée and remaining 2$1/2$ cups corn. Add the half-and-half and mix well.

Simmer just until heated through, stirring frequently. Season with salt and pepper. Ladle into soup bowls. Sprinkle with chives and parsley.

Yield: 12 servings

Ginger Carrot Soup©

Vista Clara Ranch Resort & Spa

1 large yellow onion, coarsely chopped
2 pounds carrots, chopped, or 2 pounds whole baby carrots
2 medium pieces gingerroot, peeled, coarsely chopped
Vegetable broth or water
Frozen apple juice concentrate
Sour cream or yogurt
Sprigs of dillweed or finely chopped chives

Sauté the onion in a large nonstick saucepan over medium heat until tender. Add the carrots and gingerroot; cover. Sweat the vegetables over low heat until tender-crisp and aromatic. This process helps to develop a richer flavor in the vegetables. Add equal portions of the broth and apple juice concentrate to the carrot mixture until the vegetables are covered by 1 inch of liquid.

Simmer for 40 minutes or until the carrots are very tender, stirring occasionally. Process the mixture in batches in a food processor until smooth. Ladle into soup bowls. Top each serving with a dollop of sour cream and a sprig of dillweed.

Yield: 8 servings

The Vista Clara Ranch Resort & Spa will pamper you with Southwestern-style rooms and gourmet spa cuisine. Should you so desire, explore the Native American culture and ancestral ways with a traditional sweat lodge.

Corrales Carrot Soup

6 tablespoons butter
8 medium carrots, peeled, thinly sliced
1 medium onion, thinly sliced
4 cups chicken stock
3 tablespoons uncooked white rice
$1/2$ teaspoon salt
$1/2$ teaspoon curry powder
$1/8$ teaspoon pepper
1 sprig of fresh thyme, or $1/8$ teaspoon dried thyme
Shredded cheese (optional)
Sour cream (optional)
Sunflower kernels (optional)

Heat the butter in a $2^1/2$-quart saucepan until melted. Stir in the carrots and onion. Simmer, covered, for 5 minutes, stirring occasionally. Add the stock, rice, salt, curry powder, pepper and thyme and mix well.

Simmer for 30 minutes, stirring occasionally. Discard the fresh thyme. Process the soup in a blender in 2 or 3 batches until smooth but not liquified. Return the soup to the saucepan. Cook just until heated through, stirring frequently. Ladle into soup bowls. Garnish with cheese, sour cream and/or sunflower kernels. For a thinner consistency, add 2 tablespoons butter or stock.

Yield: 4 servings

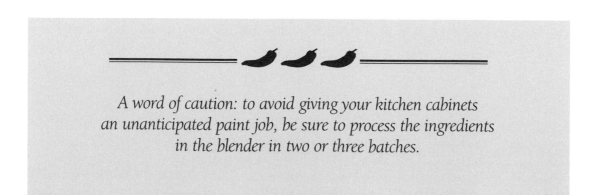

A word of caution: to avoid giving your kitchen cabinets
an unanticipated paint job, be sure to process the ingredients
in the blender in two or three batches.

Cream of Leek Soup

3 leeks, thinly sliced
1 1/2 teaspoons vegetable oil
2 garlic cloves, minced
1 1/2 teaspoons minced fresh thyme, or 1/2 teaspoon dried thyme
6 cups chicken stock
3 medium potatoes, peeled, chopped
1 1/2 cups nonfat sour cream
Salt and pepper to taste
Nonfat sour cream to taste
Sprigs of fresh thyme

Sauté the leeks in the oil in a stockpot for 10 minutes. Stir in the garlic and thyme. Sauté for 2 minutes. Stir in the stock. Bring to a boil; reduce the heat.

Simmer for 10 minutes, stirring occasionally. Strain into a bowl, reserving the stock and solids. Process the leeks in a blender until puréed.

Return the stock and leek purée to the stockpot. Stir in the potatoes. Simmer until the potatoes are tender, stirring occasionally. Remove from heat. Mash the potatoes. Stir in 1 1/2 cups sour cream. Simmer just until heated through, stirring frequently; do not boil. Ladle into soup bowls. Top each serving with sour cream to taste. Garnish with sprigs of thyme.

Yield: 4 servings

Mushroom Soup with Brie

2^1/2 cups chopped onions
3 tablespoons butter
1 pound fresh mushrooms, thinly sliced
^{3}/4 cup white wine
2 to 3 tablespoons dillweed
1^1/4 tablespoons paprika
1^1/2 tablespoons soy sauce
1 tablespoon Worcestershire sauce
3 tablespoons butter
^{1}/4 cup flour
1^1/2 cups milk
2^1/2 cups chicken broth
6 to 8 ounces Brie cheese, rind removed, cubed
1 cup sour cream
Salt and pepper to taste
^{1}/2 cup pine nuts (optional)

Cook the onions in 3 tablespoons butter in a saucepan until tender. Stir in the mushrooms, wine, dillweed, paprika, soy sauce and Worcestershire sauce. Simmer for 15 minutes, stirring occasionally.

Heat 3 tablespoons butter in a medium saucepan until melted. Stir in the flour. Cook over low heat for 3 minutes, stirring constantly. Remove from heat. Whisk in the milk until blended. Cook over medium-low heat until thickened, stirring constantly. Add the mushroom mixture and mix well. Stir in the broth. Simmer over low heat for 15 to 20 minutes, stirring occasionally. Reduce the heat to low.

Stir the Brie into the soup with a wooden spoon. Cook for 2 minutes or until the cheese melts, stirring constantly. Remove from heat. Stir in the sour cream. Season with salt and pepper. Ladle into soup bowls. Sprinkle with the pine nuts.

Yield: 8 servings

Portobello Barley Soup

4 cups water
3/4 cup pearl barley
1 tablespoon olive oil
4 onions, chopped
2 ribs celery, chopped
1 1/2 pounds portobello mushrooms, chopped
3 carrots, sliced
1/2 cup chopped fresh parsley
4 cups reduced-sodium beef or vegetable broth
2 tomatoes, chopped
3 tablespoons tomato paste
1/2 teaspoon salt
1/4 teaspoon pepper

Combine the water and barley in a saucepan. Bring to a boil; reduce heat. Simmer, partially covered, for 30 minutes or until the barley is partially cooked.

Heat the olive oil in a large heavy saucepan. Stir in the onions and celery. Cook for 8 minutes or until the vegetables are tender, stirring constantly. Add the mushrooms, carrots and parsley and mix well. Cook for 5 minutes, stirring frequently. Stir in the undrained barley, broth, tomatoes and tomato paste. Bring to a boil; reduce heat.

Simmer, partially covered, for 30 minutes or until the carrots and barley are tender, stirring occasionally. Stir in the salt and pepper. Ladle into soup bowls. Serve with crusty French bread.

Yield: 6 servings

Red Pepper Soup with Cumin Cream

From Rancho de San Juan

Soup
3 pounds red bell peppers
1 jalapeño chile
3 tablespoons butter
1/2 cup flour
4 cups rich chicken stock, preferably homemade
Salt to taste

Cumin Cream
2 tablespoons cumin seeds
1 cup sour cream
1 cup heavy cream

For the soup, grill the bell peppers over an open gas flame until the skins are blistered and charred on all sides, turning frequently; do not burn. Place the bell peppers in a sealable plastic bag and seal tightly. Allow to steam in the bag for 30 minutes or until cooled. Peel, seed and chop the bell peppers when cool. Wear rubber or plastic gloves to protect your hands from the pepper oils. Process the bell peppers in a blender until puréed. Repeat the process with the jalapeño chile.

Heat the butter in a saucepan until melted. Stir in the flour. Cook for 2 minutes, stirring constantly. Add the stock and mix well. Simmer until thickened and of the consistency of heavy cream, stirring constantly and adding additional stock if needed for the desired consistency. Fold in the puréed peppers.

Simmer just until heated through, stirring constantly. Season with salt. Ladle into soup bowls.

For the cream, toast the cumin seeds in a skillet just until they begin to color. Grind into a powder. Combine the ground cumin with the sour cream and heavy cream in a bowl and mix well. Pour into a plastic squeeze bottle. Decorate the top of each serving as desired.

Yield: 4 servings

Indian Yellow Split Pea Soup

From The Artichoke Café

1 pound dried yellow split peas
1 bunch cilantro
3 tablespoons ghee or clarified butter
3 red onions, chopped
4 ribs celery, chopped
3 carrots, peeled, chopped
5 garlic cloves, minced
1 (1-inch-piece) gingerroot, peeled, grated
1 tablespoon garam masala
1 tablespoon coriander seeds, crushed
1 teaspoon paprika
1 teaspoon turmeric
8 cups vegetable stock
1 teaspoon kosher salt

Sort and rinse the peas. Separate the leaves and stems of the cilantro and chop separately. Heat the ghee in a stockpot over medium heat until melted. Add the onions, celery and carrots and mix well. Sauté until caramelized. Stir in the garlic, gingerroot, and cilantro stems.

Cook for 1 minute, stirring occasionally. Add the garam masala, coriander seeds, paprika and turmeric and mix well. Cook for 3 to 5 minutes, stirring occasionally. Stir in the peas and stock. Bring to a boil; reduce the heat.

Simmer, covered, until the peas are tender, stirring occasionally. Add the kosher salt and mix well. Ladle into soup bowls. Sprinkle with the cilantro leaves. Ghee and garam masala are available at East Indian specialty markets.

Yield: 6 to 8 servings

Jamaican Pumpkin Soup

1 medium pumpkin, or 2 cups canned pumpkin
2 quarts chicken broth
1 bunch green onions, chopped
1/4 cup flaked coconut
1/2 teaspoon thyme
1/2 teaspoon salt
3/4 teaspoon Tabasco sauce
Freshly ground pepper to taste

Peel, seed and chop the pumpkin. Combine 2 pounds of the chopped pumpkin, broth, green onions, coconut, thyme and salt in a stockpot. Bring to a boil; reduce heat.
Simmer for 45 minutes or until the pumpkin is tender, stirring occasionally. Process the soup in batches in a blender or food processor until puréed. Return the soup to the stockpot. Stir in the Tabasco sauce and pepper. Simmer just until heated through, stirring frequently. Ladle into soup bowls.

Yield: 8 servings

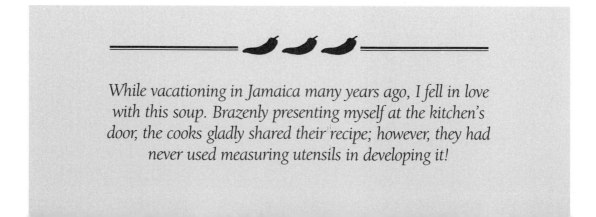

While vacationing in Jamaica many years ago, I fell in love with this soup. Brazenly presenting myself at the kitchen's door, the cooks gladly shared their recipe; however, they had never used measuring utensils in developing it!

Butternut Squash and Ginger Soup

1¹/2 cups chopped yellow onions
4 garlic cloves, chopped
3 tablespoons olive oil
4 cups sliced peeled butternut squash
1 teaspoon coriander
1/4 teaspoon cinnamon
4 cups water
1/4 cup grated gingerroot
1 tablespoon soy sauce
Salt and pepper to taste
Chopped fresh cilantro

Sauté the onions and garlic in the olive oil in a large saucepan until the onions are tender. Stir in the squash, coriander and cinnamon. Cook for 5 minutes, stirring occasionally. Add the water and mix well.

Simmer for 1 hour, stirring occasionally. Stir in the gingerroot and soy sauce. Process the soup in batches in a food processor until smooth. Return the soup to the saucepan. Cook just until heated through, stirring frequently. Season with salt and pepper. Ladle into soup bowls. Top with cilantro.

Yield: 4 to 6 servings

Zucchini Chowder

2 medium zucchini, chopped
1 medium onion, chopped
2 tablespoons minced fresh parsley
1 teaspoon basil
1/3 cup butter or margarine
1/3 cup flour
1 teaspoon salt
Pepper to taste
3 cups water
3 chicken bouillon cubes
1 teaspoon lemon juice
1 (14-ounce) can diced tomatoes
1 (12-ounce) can evaporated milk
1 (10-ounce) package frozen whole kernel corn
2 cups shredded Cheddar cheese
1/4 cup grated Parmesan cheese

Sauté the zucchini, onion, parsley and basil in the butter in a large saucepan until the zucchini and onion are tender. Stir in the flour, salt and pepper. Add the water gradually, stirring constantly. Add the bouillon cubes and lemon juice and mix well. Bring to a boil.

Cook for 2 minutes, stirring constantly. Stir in the undrained tomatoes, evaporated milk and corn. Reduce the heat. Simmer, covered, for 5 minutes, stirring occasionally. Add the Cheddar cheese and Parmesan cheese just before serving and stir until melted. Ladle into soup bowls. For a Southwestern flavor, add a can of chopped green chiles or substitute the diced tomatoes with a can of tomatoes and green chiles.

Yield: 8 to 10 servings

Santa Fe Gazpacho

From The Bishop's Lodge

1 (32-ounce) can diced tomatoes
1 (32-ounce) can vegetable juice cocktail
2 poblano chiles, seeded, minced
1 small red bell pepper, finely chopped
1 small yellow bell pepper, finely chopped
3 small fresh jalapeño chiles, seeded, minced

1 small red onion, finely chopped
1 cucumber, peeled, seeded, finely chopped
1/2 cup red wine vinegar
1/4 bunch cilantro, trimmed, finely chopped
1/4 cup extra-virgin olive oil
1/2 teaspoon minced garlic
Salt and pepper to taste
Julienned cucumber
Red chile croutons

Combine the undrained tomatoes and vegetable juice cocktail in a 2-gallon metal container and mix well. Place the metal container in an ice bath. Stir in the poblano chiles, bell peppers, jalapeño chiles, onion and chopped cucumber. Add the wine vinegar, cilantro, olive oil and garlic and mix well. Season with salt and pepper. Store in the ice bath. Ladle into chilled soup bowls just before serving. Top with julienned cucumber and/or red chile croutons.

Yield: 1 1/4 gallons soup

The Bishop's Lodge is nestled in the scenic village of Tesuque, just outside of Santa Fe. Always a favorite destination, we are pleased to share their version of gazpacho.

Tortilla Soup

From The Bishop's Lodge

2 tablespoons corn oil
2 medium Spanish onions, chopped
2 large fresh jalapeño chiles, chopped
2 ancho chiles, chopped
4 garlic cloves, minced
1 gallon chicken stock
3 cups tomato juice
4 teaspoons coriander
4 teaspoons cumin
3/4 bunch cilantro, trimmed, chopped
Juice of 2 limes
Salt and pepper to taste
5 ears corn, grilled, shucked
15 BUENO® corn tortillas, heated

Heat the corn oil in a stockpot until very hot. Add the onions, jalapeño chiles, ancho chiles and garlic and mix well. Sauté for 10 minutes or until the vegetables and chiles are tender. Stir in the stock and tomato juice. Bring to a boil, stirring frequently to prevent the vegetables from sticking to the bottom. Reduce the heat.

Simmer for 1 hour, stirring occasionally. Stir in the coriander, cumin and cilantro. Process the soup in batches in a food processor or blender until smooth. Stir in the lime juice, salt and pepper. Process again until puréed. Return the soup to the stockpot. Remove the corn kernels from the cob and add to the soup. Simmer just until heated through, stirring frequently. Ladle into soup bowls. Serve with the warm tortillas.

Yield: 5 quarts

New Mexican Cheese Soup

2 large white onions, chopped
1/2 cup (1 stick) butter
3/4 cup flour
6 cups chicken broth
2 pounds Jalapeño-Jack cheese, shredded
6 boneless skinless chicken breasts, chopped
2 cups milk

1/3 cup chopped BUENO® frozen green chile
1 teaspoon salt
1 teaspoon pepper
4 to 6 potatoes, coarsely chopped (optional)
Tortilla chips
8 ounces longhorn cheese, shredded

Sauté the onions in the butter in a stockpot until tender. Add the flour gradually, stirring constantly until the onions are coated. Add the broth 1 cup a time, mixing well after each addition. Stir in the Jalapeño-Jack cheese, chicken, milk, green chile, salt and pepper. Bring to a boil, stirring constantly.

Boil until the cheese melts, stirring constantly. Reduce the heat. Simmer for 1 hour, stirring occasionally. Stir in the potatoes. Simmer for 1 hour longer, stirring occasionally.

Crumble the tortilla chips over the bottom of 10 to 12 soup bowls. Ladle the hot soup over the chips. Sprinkle with the longhorn cheese. Serve immediately.

Yield: 10 to 12 servings

For a heart-healthy version of New Mexican Cheese Soup, decrease the butter to 1/4 cup and use fat-free chicken broth, reduced-fat or skim milk, salt substitute, and baked tortilla chips.

Green Chile Chicken Soup

2 pounds chicken breasts
6 cups water
1 tablespoon salt
1 large onion,
finely chopped
2 garlic cloves, minced
2 cups BUENO® frozen green chile
2 tablespoons flour
16 ounces cream cheese
2 cups half-and-half

Combine the chicken, water and salt in a stockpot. Bring to a boil. Boil until the chicken is tender. Remove the chicken to a platter with a slotted spoon, reserving the stock. Add the onion and garlic to the boiling stock. Cook for 15 minutes or until the onion is tender.

Chop the chicken into bite-size pieces, discarding the skin and bones. Add the chicken and green chile to the boiling broth. Scoop out 1 cup of the boiling broth. Let cool for 15 minutes. Stir the flour into the 1 cup broth until blended. Add the flour mixture to the boiling stock and mix well. Cook for 15 minutes, stirring frequently.

Place the cream cheese in a microwave-safe dish. Microwave on High for 2 minutes or until softened. Add the half-and-half gradually to the cream cheese, whisking constantly until blended. Add the cream cheese mixture gradually to the boiling stock, stirring constantly. Reduce the heat to simmer.

Simmer for 10 minutes, stirring occasionally; do not boil. Ladle into soup bowls.

Yield: 6 to 8 servings

Blanco Chili

1 tablespoon olive oil
1 pound boneless skinless chicken breasts, chopped
$1/2$ cup chopped onion
$1^1/2$ cups chicken broth
$1/2$ cup BUENO® frozen green chile
1 teaspoon garlic powder
1 teaspoon cumin
$1/2$ teaspoon oregano
$1/2$ teaspoon cilantro
$1/4$ teaspoon ground red pepper
1 (19-ounce) can cannellini or Great Northern beans

Heat the olive oil in a 2- or 3-quart saucepan over medium-high heat. Stir in the chicken. Sauté for 4 to 5 minutes or until cooked through. Remove the chicken with a slotted spoon to a bowl, reserving the pan drippings. Stir the onion into the reserved pan drippings.

Cook for 2 minutes, stirring constantly. Stir in the broth, green chiles, garlic powder, cumin, oregano, cilantro and red pepper. Simmer for 30 minutes, stirring occasionally. Stir in the chicken and undrained beans. Simmer just until heated through, stirring frequently. Ladle into soup bowls.

As an alternative, combine the cooked chicken and sautéed onions with the remaining ingredients in a slow cooker and mix well. Cook on Medium for 2 to 3 hours or on Low for 5 to 6 hours.

Yield: 4 servings

For a buffet serve Blanco Chili with the following condiments: guacamole, chopped tomatoes, chopped fresh parsley, chopped black olives, sour cream and/or crumbled tortilla chips.

Male Chauvinist Chili

3 slices bacon, chopped
8 ounces hot Italian link
sausage, cut into 1-inch slices
1 to 1¹/₂ pounds
ground chuck
2 medium onions, chopped
2 garlic cloves, minced
1 jalapeño chile, minced
2 (16-ounce) cans Italian
tomatoes

1 (16-ounce) can kidney
beans
1 tablespoon BUENO®
chile powder
2 teaspoons Worcestershire
sauce
¹/₂ teaspoon dry mustard
¹/₄ teaspoon ground pepper
³/₄ cup sherry

Fry the bacon in a skillet until crisp. Remove the bacon to a bowl with a slotted spoon, discarding the pan drippings. Add the sausage, ground chuck, onions, garlic and jalapeño chile to the skillet. Cook over medium heat until the sausage is brown and the ground chuck is brown and crumbly, stirring constantly; drain. Spoon the sausage mixture into a slow cooker.

Add the bacon, undrained tomatoes, undrained kidney beans, chile powder, Worcestershire sauce, dry mustard and pepper to the slow cooker and mix well. Cook on Low for 8 to 14 hours or until of the desired consistency, stirring occasionally. Stir in the sherry just before serving. Ladle into soup bowls.

Yield: 6 servings

*One of our testers reported, "I had marriage proposals when
I served this chili at an office luncheon!"*

Pork and Green Chile Stew

2 tablespoons vegetable oil
2¹/₂ pounds pork from a pork roast or
country-style ribs, cut into cubes
3 cups water
³/₄ cup BUENO® frozen green chile
3 potatoes, chopped
1 (15-ounce) can whole kernel corn
¹/₃ cup chopped onion
1 (15-ounce) can diced tomatoes
2 cups large zucchini pieces

Heat the oil in a Dutch oven over medium-high heat until hot. Brown the pork in the hot oil. Add the water and bring to a simmer. Simmer for 1 hour. Add the green chile, potatoes, corn, onion and tomatoes. Simmer for 1³/₄ hours. Add the zucchini. Simmer for 15 minutes or until zucchini is tender.

Yield: 6 servings

Mí Casa Sausage Soup

1½ pounds bulk Italian sausage,
casings removed, crumbled
2 large onions, chopped
1 green bell pepper, chopped
2 garlic cloves, minced
1 (28-ounce) can diced or crushed tomatoes
4 cups beef broth
1½ cups dry red wine
3 tablespoons chopped fresh parsley, or
1 tablespoon parsley flakes
½ teaspoon dried basil, crushed
½ teaspoon dried oregano, crushed
8 ounces spaghettini, broken
Grated Parmesan cheese

Cook the sausage in a 5-quart Dutch oven over medium heat until the sausage is no longer pink, stirring frequently. Stir in the onions, bell pepper and garlic. Cook until the onions and bell pepper are tender, stirring constantly. Add the undrained tomatoes and mix well. Stir in the broth, wine, parsley, basil and oregano.

Simmer for 30 minutes, stirring occasionally. Add the pasta and mix well. Simmer for 25 minutes longer or until the pasta is tender, stirring occasionally. Ladle into soup bowls. Serve with Parmesan cheese.

Yield: 6 to 8 servings

Lamb and Bean Stew

4 (1-pound) lamb shanks
2 tablespoons flour
3 tablespoons vegetable oil
1 medium onion, chopped
1 large rib celery, chopped
1 (14- to 16-ounce) can stewed tomatoes
1 (13- to 14-ounce) can beef broth
1 garlic clove, minced
1 bay leaf
1/2 teaspoon dried thyme
1/2 teaspoon salt
1/4 teaspoon coarsely ground pepper
1 (16- to 19-ounce) can Great Northern beans, drained
Mashed potatoes
1 teaspoon chopped fresh parsley
1 teaspoon grated lemon zest

Coat the lamb shanks with the flour. Heat the oil in a 5-quart Dutch oven over medium-high heat until hot. Add the lamb. Cook until brown on all sides, turning frequently. Remove the lamb to a bowl with a slotted spoon, reserving the pan drippings.

Sauté the onion and celery in the reserved pan drippings over medium heat until brown. Return the lamb to the Dutch oven. Stir in the undrained tomatoes, broth, garlic, bay leaf, thyme, salt and pepper. Bring to a boil over high heat.

Bake, covered, at 350 degrees for 1 1/2 hours or until the lamb is tender, turning once. Remove from the oven.

Skim the fat from the surface of the liquid. Stir in the beans. Cook just until heated through, stirring frequently. Discard the bay leaf. Spoon the desired amount of mashed potatoes into each of 6 bowls. Ladle the stew over the potatoes. Sprinkle with the parsley and lemon zest.

Yield: 6 servings

Sandia Sunrises
Breads and Brunch

Touching the Skies

As the morning sun gently rises above the Sandia Mountains, skies are often filled with the vivid colors of hot air balloons. Ballooning is a peaceful sport, one that relies on a silent, effortless force that gently pulls each creative behemoth from its earthly bonds. Propelled by the same gentle rise, the balloons can also drift down to softly dash the waters of the Rio Grande.

Tradition dictates that if a hot air balloon lands in a yard, its occupants must present the resident with a bottle of Champagne to be opened at once and enjoyed together.

Due to favorable winds and climate, New Mexico is the world's most desirable locale for hot air ballooning. October beckons balloonists from around the world, who set skies ablaze with their huge, gentle giants. From the first weekend through the second weekend each October, hundreds of thousands of people converge upon Albuquerque to surround themselves with the excitement of this mystical sport.

Waking long before dawn, balloonists and their crews look forward to packing up their gear and pondering the resplendent southwestern brunch. Ranging from distinctive cuisine such as huevos rancheros to a sweet blend of eggs, sausage, and other treats wrapped in a warm flour tortilla, New Mexican brunches offer a time of peacefulness, camaraderie, and distinctive cuisine.

GRUET

Make-Ahead Brunch

For After the Balloons

French Toast with Orange and Pecans

Sunrise Egg Soufflé

Cinnamon Maple Pears

Graham Streusel Coffee Cake

Serve with a lightly flavored coffee and mimosas.

Savor the Morning

Brunch for Any Season

Blue Cornmeal Crepes with Chicken

Sicilian Spinach Pie

Black Bean Tart

Red Hot Cheese Biscuits

Bread Pudding

Make a batch of Gringo Red Chile Sauce for a colorful accompaniment.

Cinnamon Peach Bread

2 cups flour
1 teaspoon cinnamon
1 teaspoon baking soda
1 teaspoon baking powder
$1/4$ teaspoon salt
$1/2$ cup sugar

$1/2$ cup vegetable oil
2 cups peach purée
2 eggs
1 cup chopped walnuts
1 teaspoon vanilla extract

Mix the flour, cinnamon, baking soda, baking powder and salt in a bowl. Beat the sugar and oil in a mixing bowl until creamy. Add the peach purée and eggs and beat until blended. Add the flour mixture and mix well. Stir in the walnuts and vanilla.

Spoon the batter into 2 greased and floured 5×9-inch loaf pans. Bake at 325 degrees for 1 hour. Cool in pans for 10 minutes. Remove to a wire rack to cool completely. Six to seven medium peaches is equal to 2 cups purée.

Yield: 24 servings

Toasted Coconut Bread

1 cup shredded coconut
3 cups sifted flour
$1^1/2$ cups sugar
1 teaspoon baking powder

$1/2$ teaspoon salt
1 egg
$1^1/2$ cups milk
1 teaspoon vanilla extract

Spread the coconut on a baking sheet. Toast at 350 degrees until light brown, stirring occasionally. Sift the flour, sugar, baking powder and salt into a bowl and mix well. Stir in the coconut. Beat the egg in a mixing bowl until foamy. Add the milk and vanilla and beat until blended. Add the milk mixture to the flour mixture and mix just until moistened. Spoon the batter into a 5×9-inch loaf pan sprayed with nonstick cooking spray. Bake at 350 degrees for 60 to 70 minutes or until the loaf tests done. Cool in the pan for 10 minutes. Remove to a wire rack to cool completely.

Yield: 12 servings

Jalapeño Corn Bread

From PNM's Cocinas de New Mexico

1 cup flour	1/4 cup shortening
1 cup yellow cornmeal	2 eggs
1/4 cup sugar	1 (8-ounce) can
1 tablespoon baking powder	cream-style corn
1 teaspoon salt	2 tablespoons chopped
1/4 teaspoon garlic powder	jalapeños or BUENO®
1 cup milk	frozen green chile

Combine the flour, cornmeal, sugar, baking powder, salt and garlic powder in a mixing bowl and mix well. Add the milk, shortening and eggs.

Beat until smooth, scraping the bowl occasionally. Add the corn and jalapeño chiles and mix well. Spoon the batter into a greased 8×8-inch baking pan. Bake at 425 degrees for 35 to 40 minutes or until golden brown. Adjust the amount of chiles to taste.

Yield: 16 (1-inch) squares

Red Hot Cheese Biscuits

2 3/4 cups baking mix	1 cup shredded Cheddar
1/2 teaspoon BUENO®	cheese
crushed red chile	2 tablespoons butter, melted
1/4 teaspoon garlic powder	1/4 teaspoon garlic powder
1 cup milk	

Combine the baking mix, red pepper and 1/4 teaspoon garlic powder in a bowl and mix well. Add the milk and cheese and stir with a fork until a soft dough forms. Drop the dough onto a baking sheet in 1/4-cup increments. Combine the butter and 1/4 teaspoon garlic powder in a bowl and mix well. Brush the butter mixture over the tops of the biscuits. Bake at 425 degrees for 10 to 12 minutes or until golden brown.

Yield: 1 dozen biscuits

Yummy Yam Biscuits

From Doc Martin's Restaurant at The Historic Taos Inn

3 cups flour
1/4 cup sugar
2 tablespoons baking powder
1 teaspoon salt
1 cup shortening
3 cups mashed cooked yams
1/2 cup milk

Sift the flour, sugar, baking powder and salt into a bowl and mix well. Cut in the shortening until crumbly. Whisk the yams and milk in a large bowl until blended. Add to the flour mixture and mix well.

Shape the dough into 2-inch balls. Arrange 2 inches apart on a greased baking sheet. Bake at 350 degrees until the biscuits test done and are golden brown.

Yield: 20 biscuits

We top our Yummy Yam Biscuits with poached eggs, red chile sauce, and melted cheese and it has been on the menu forever. We call it the Kit Carson, and the sweet from the yam plays off the heat of the red chile and it is delicious. See page 194 for the Red Chile Sauce.

Cheese Blintz Muffins

From Cinnamon Morning Bed & Breakfast

Muffins
2 cups part-skim ricotta cheese
1/2 cup baking mix
1/3 cup sugar
1/4 cup (1/2 stick) butter, melted
3 eggs, lightly beaten
2 tablespoons sour cream or yogurt
1 tablespoon vanilla extract

Blueberry Sauce and Assembly
1 tablespoon cornstarch
1/3 cup warm water
1/3 cup sugar
2 tablespoons lemon juice
2 cups fresh or frozen blueberries
Sour cream

For the muffins, combine the ricotta cheese, baking mix, sugar, butter, eggs, sour cream and vanilla in a bowl and mix well. Spoon the batter into 12 greased muffin cups. Bake at 350 degrees for 30 minutes or until light brown.

For the sauce, dissolve the cornstarch in the warm water and mix well. Combine the cornstarch mixture, sugar and lemon juice in a saucepan and mix well. Stir in the blueberries. Cook over medium heat until thickened, stirring constantly.

To assemble, arrange 2 muffins on each plate. Drizzle with the warm sauce. Top with a dollop of sour cream.

Yield: 6 servings

Cinnamon Coffee Cakes

2 cups flour
1¹/₂ cups sugar
2 teaspoons cinnamon
¹/₈ teaspoon salt
¹/₂ cup (1 stick) butter,
cut into pieces, chilled
1 cup chopped walnuts or pecans
1 egg, beaten
1 cup buttermilk
1 teaspoon baking soda

Combine the flour, sugar, cinnamon and salt in a bowl and mix well. Cut in the butter until crumbly. Stir in the walnuts. Reserve ¹/₂ cup of the crumb mixture.

Combine the remaining crumb mixture with the egg and mix well. Combine the buttermilk and baking soda in a small bowl and mix well. Add to the egg mixture and mix well. Spoon the batter into 2 greased 8-inch round baking pans. Sprinkle with the reserved crumb mixture.

Bake at 350 degrees for 25 to 30 minutes or until the coffee cakes test done. These coffee cakes may be baked in disposable aluminum pie pans and frozen, covered, for future use. Thaw at room temperature or in the refrigerator for 8 to 10 hours.

Yield: 12 servings

Graham Streusel Coffee Cake

Streusel
1 1/2 cups graham cracker crumbs (about 21 crackers)
3/4 cup chopped pecans or walnuts
3/4 cup packed light brown sugar
1 1/2 teaspoons cinnamon
2/3 cup butter or margarine, melted

Coffee Cake
1 (2-layer) package yellow or white cake mix
1 cup water
1/4 cup vegetable oil
3 eggs
Confectioners' sugar icing

For the streusel, combine the graham cracker crumbs, pecans, brown sugar and cinnamon in a bowl and mix well. Stir in the butter.

For the coffee cake, combine the cake mix, water, oil and eggs in a mixing bowl. Beat at low speed just until moistened, scraping the bowl occasionally. Beat at medium speed for 1 minute. Layer the batter and streusel 1/2 at a time in a greased 9×13-inch baking pan.

Bake at 350 degrees for 35 to 40 minutes or until a wooden pick inserted in the center comes out clean. Cool slightly. Drizzle with a confectioners' sugar icing. Serve warm.

Yield: 12 to 16 servings

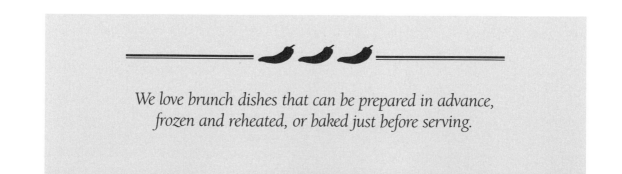

*We love brunch dishes that can be prepared in advance,
frozen and reheated, or baked just before serving.*

Blue Cornmeal Crepes with Chicken

Olas de Crema con Pollo

From Bueno Foods

Crepes

¹/₂ cup BUENO® blue cornmeal
¹/₂ cup whole wheat flour
¹/₂ teaspoon salt
³/₄ cup milk
¹/₄ cup vegetable oil

¹/₂ cup BUENO® frozen mild or
hot green chile, thawed, drained
1 egg, lightly beaten
1 teaspoon olive oil

Chicken Filling and Assembly

¹/₂ cup finely chopped onion
1 garlic clove, minced
1 tablespoon butter or
margarine
1 cup shredded
cooked chicken
(about 1 chicken breast)

¹/₂ cup BUENO® frozen
green chile, thawed, drained
1 small tomato, chopped
1 cup light cream
2 chicken bouillon cubes
¹/₂ cup shredded Cheddar
cheese

For the crepes, combine the cornmeal, whole wheat flour and salt in a bowl and mix well. Stir in the milk, vegetable oil, green chile and egg. Pour the olive oil into a small bowl. Dip a paper towel into the olive oil and lightly grease a small nonstick skillet prior to cooking each crepe. Heat the skillet over medium-high heat until almost smoking. Pour 3 tablespoons of the crepe batter into the hot skillet, tilting the pan to cover the bottom evenly. Cook over medium heat for 1 minute or until brown; turn. Cook for 30 seconds longer or until brown. Repeat the process with the remaining olive oil and batter.

For the filling, sauté the onion and garlic in the butter in a saucepan. Stir in the chicken, green chile and tomato. Cook, covered, over medium heat for 10 minutes, stirring occasionally.

To assemble, fill each crepe with 2 tablespoons of the chicken filling. Roll to enclose the filling. Arrange the crepes seam side down in a lightly greased 8×10-inch baking dish. Heat the light cream in a saucepan over low heat. Add the bouillon cubes. Simmer until blended, stirring constantly. Spoon over the crepes. Sprinkle with the cheese. Bake at 350 degrees for 15 minutes or until the cheese melts.

Yield: 10 crepes

French Toast with Orange and Pecans

1 (12-ounce) loaf dry French bread, thickly sliced
2/3 cup orange juice
1/3 cup milk
1/4 cup sugar
4 eggs
1/2 teaspoon vanilla extract
1/4 teaspoon nutmeg
1/3 cup butter
1/2 cup pecan halves, toasted
2 tablespoons grated orange zest

Arrange the bread slices in a single layer in a large shallow dish. Blend the orange juice, milk, sugar, eggs, vanilla and nutmeg in a bowl. Pour over the bread. Chill, covered, for 8 to 10 hours. Remove the dish from the refrigerator 30 minutes before baking. Melt the butter in a baking pan, tilting the pan to cover the bottom evenly. Arrange the bread slices in a single layer in the prepared pan. Sprinkle with the pecan halves and orange zest. Bake at 400 degrees for 20 to 25 minutes or until light brown. Serve with maple syrup or fresh fruit.

Yield: 4 servings

Pumpkin Pancakes

From Hacienda Vargas Bed & Breakfast Inn & Chapel

2 cups baking mix
2 teaspoons brown sugar
1 teaspoon cinnamon
1 teaspoon allspice
1/2 (16-ounce) can pumpkin
1 (12-ounce) can evaporated milk
2 eggs, lightly beaten
2 teaspoons vegetable oil
1 teaspoon vanilla extract

Combine the baking mix, brown sugar, cinnamon and allspice in a bowl and mix well. Add the pumpkin, evaporated milk, eggs, oil and vanilla, stirring until smooth.

Pour approximately 1/4 cup of the batter onto a hot lightly oiled griddle. Cook until brown on both sides. Repeat with the remaining batter. Serve with syrup or honey.

Yield: 16 pancakes

Garlic Cheese Grits

From Los Poblanos Inn

4 cups water
1 cup instant grits
1/2 cup (1 stick) butter
1 (6-ounce) roll garlic jalapeño cheese
1 garlic clove, crushed
1 egg
1 cup (scant) milk, heated
1 cup shredded Monterey Jack or Cheddar cheese
1/2 teaspoon paprika

Bring the water to a boil in a saucepan. Stir in the grits. Cook for 3 minutes. Remove from heat. Stir in the butter, garlic jalapeño cheese and garlic. Cover and set aside.

Whisk the egg and warm milk in a bowl. Stir into the grits mixture. Spoon into a lightly oiled baking dish. Sprinkle with the Monterey Jack cheese and paprika. Bake at 350 degrees for 1 hour. Serve immediately.

Yield: 4 to 6 servings

We used to have a Christmas Day brunch when we lived in the old Lovelace House. You were supposed to bring your children, houseguests and anyone who usually spent Christmas with you as well as your ugliest present to exchange. I realized it was out of hand when one year a couple brought a moose head! They had to come in a convertible. Some people actually shopped for ugly things to bring but strangely enough, by the end of the afternoon, all the gifts were exchanged, which proves that beauty is in the eye of the beholder or, there's no accounting for bad taste.

Black Bean Tart

1¹/2 cups sour cream
1 tablespoon (or more) fresh lime juice
1¹/4 cups flour
1 teaspoon cumin
1 teaspoon BUENO® chile powder
1 teaspoon paprika
¹/2 teaspoon salt
¹/2 cup (1 stick) unsalted butter, sliced, chilled
2 tablespoons ice water
4 cups canned black beans, rinsed, drained

Salt and pepper to taste
Vegetable oil
1 (10-ounce) package frozen corn, thawed, drained
1¹/2 cups shredded Monterey Jack cheese
1 red bell pepper, chopped
¹/2 cup chopped fresh cilantro
¹/2 cup chopped scallions
2 fresh jalapeño chiles, seeded, finely chopped

Combine 1 cup of the sour cream and lime juice in a bowl and mix well. You may prepare 1 day in advance and store, covered, in the refrigerator.

Pulse the flour, cumin, chile powder, paprika and ¹/2 teaspoon salt in a food processor until combined. Add the butter. Process until crumbly. Add the ice water. Pulse until the mixture forms a ball. Press the pastry evenly over the bottom and up the side of a 10-inch tart pan with a removable fluted rim. Chill for 15 minutes or until firm. Line the pastry with foil and weight with dried beans.

Bake at 350 degrees for 10 minutes or until the edge is set. Remove the beans and foil. Bake for 10 minutes longer or until golden brown. Let stand until cool. You may prepare 1 day in advance and store, loosely covered, at room temperature.

Process 1 cup of the beans and the remaining ¹/2 cup sour cream in a food processor until puréed. Season with salt and pepper. Set aside. Pour enough oil into a skillet to cover the bottom. Heat over medium-high heat until hot but not smoking. Add the corn. Season with salt and pepper. Sauté for 3 minutes. Let stand until cool. Combine the corn, remaining 3 cups beans, Monterey Jack cheese, bell pepper, cilantro, scallions, jalapeño chiles and salt and pepper to taste in a bowl and mix well.

Spread the bean purée evenly over the crust. Mound with the corn mixture and press gently. Bake at 350 degrees for 20 minutes or until heated through. Cool in pan on a wire rack for 15 minutes. Remove the rim of the pan. Serve warm or at room temperature with the lime sour cream.

Yield: 8 servings

Sicilian Spinach Pie

2 (10-ounce) packages frozen chopped spinach
2 small onions, finely chopped
3 tablespoons olive oil
1 cup ricotta cheese
1 1/2 cups grated Parmesan cheese
4 eggs, lightly beaten
Salt and pepper to taste
1 unbaked (9-inch) pie shell

Cook the spinach using package directions; drain. Press the excess moisture from the spinach. Sauté the onions in the olive oil in a skillet until tender. Stir in the spinach. Let stand until cool. Add the ricotta cheese, Parmesan cheese and eggs to the spinach mixture and mix well. Season with salt and pepper. Spoon into the pie shell. Bake at 425 degrees for 40 minutes or until set.

Yield: 8 servings

Southwestern Crustless Quiche

1/2 cup (1 stick) butter
1/2 cup flour
6 extra-large eggs
1 pound Monterey Jack cheese, cubed or shredded
2 cups cottage cheese
1 cup milk
3 ounces cream cheese, softened
1 teaspoon baking powder
1 teaspoon salt
1/4 teaspoon (scant) white pepper
2 (14-ounce) cans artichoke hearts, drained, chopped

Heat the butter in a saucepan until melted. Stir in the flour. Cook over medium-low heat until smooth, stirring constantly. Whisk the eggs in a bowl until blended. Stir in the flour mixture, Monterey Jack cheese, cottage cheese, milk, cream cheese, baking powder, salt and white pepper. Arrange the chopped artichokes over the bottom of a greased 9×13-inch baking pan. Spoon the cheese mixture over the top. Bake at 350 degrees for 45 minutes.

Yield: 6 to 8 servings

Tortilla Morning

From Yours Truly Bed & Breakfast

10 BUENO® soft corn tortillas, cut into quarters
12 eggs
1/2 cup half-and-half or milk
1 (11-ounce) can Mexicorn, drained
1 cup shredded Cheddar or Monterey Jack cheese
2 cups BUENO® salsa
1 cup sour cream
1 cup guacamole

Arrange the tortillas over the bottom of a generously greased 9×13-inch baking dish. Whisk the eggs and half-and-half in a bowl until blended. Stir in the corn. Pour the egg mixture over the tortillas. Sprinkle with the cheese. Chill, covered, for 8 to 10 hours.

Bake, covered with foil, at 375 degrees for 25 to 30 minutes or just until the eggs are set. Let stand, covered, for 5 minutes. Spread with the salsa. Serve immediately with the sour cream and guacamole.

Yield: 12 to 15 servings

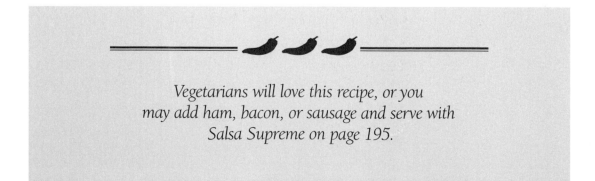

Vegetarians will love this recipe, or you may add ham, bacon, or sausage and serve with Salsa Supreme on page 195.

Sunrise Egg Soufflé

From Cinnamon Morning Bed & Breakfast

1 pound Monterey Jack cheese, shredded
2 cups reduced-fat cottage cheese
1 cup milk
1 cup flour
1/2 cup (1 stick) butter, melted
6 eggs
Croissant or bread crumbs
Fresh fruit or topping of your choice

Sprinkle the Monterey Jack cheese over the bottom of a greased 9×9-inch baking pan. Combine the cottage cheese, milk, flour, butter and eggs in a blender or food processor container. Process until smooth. Pour the egg mixture into the prepared baking pan. Sprinkle with the crumbs.

Bake at 350 degrees for 45 minutes. Cut into squares and serve with fresh fruit or your favorite topping. Cinnamon Morning's favorite toppings are apricot purée, sliced fresh peaches, sliced strawberries and New Mexico Red Chile.

Yield: 4 to 6 servings

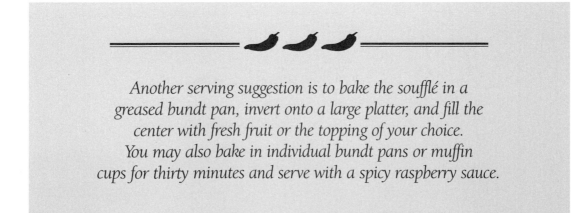

Another serving suggestion is to bake the soufflé in a greased bundt pan, invert onto a large platter, and fill the center with fresh fruit or the topping of your choice. You may also bake in individual bundt pans or muffin cups for thirty minutes and serve with a spicy raspberry sauce.

Eggs and More

From Hacienda Vargas Bed & Breakfast Inn & Chapel

1/2 cup sliced green onions
1/2 cup sliced mushrooms
1/2 cup chopped green bell pepper
3 tablespoons butter
1 cup thinly sliced ham, beef or salami
12 eggs, lightly beaten
3 tablespoons butter
3 tablespoons flour
1 1/2 to 2 cups milk
1 cup shredded cheese
1 teaspoon salt
1 1/2 cups bread crumbs
3 tablespoons butter, melted
1/2 teaspoon paprika

Sauté the green onions, mushrooms and bell pepper in 3 tablespoons butter in a skillet. Stir in the ham. Add the eggs and cook until soft scrambled. Spoon the egg mixture into a greased 9×12-inch baking pan.

Heat 3 tablespoons butter in a saucepan until melted. Stir in the flour. Cook over low heat until blended, stirring constantly. Remove from heat. Stir in the milk. Bring to a boil, stirring constantly. Boil until thickened, stirring constantly. Add the cheese and salt and mix well. Spread over the prepared layer. Sprinkle with the bread crumbs and drizzle with 3 tablespoons melted butter. Sprinkle with the paprika.

Chill, covered, for 8 to 10 hours; remove cover. Bake at 350 degrees for 30 to 40 minutes or until brown and bubbly. This recipe may be doubled for a large crowd.

Yield: 6 to 8 servings

Santa Fe Egg Casserole

1 pound bulk sausage, crumbled
12 eggs
2 cups milk
1 teaspoon salt
1 teaspoon dry mustard
1/4 cup BUENO® frozen green chile, drained

1 package frozen hash brown potatoes
1 pound Cheddar cheese, shredded
1 (2-ounce) can sliced black olives, drained (optional)

Fry the sausage in a skillet until brown and cooked through; drain. Whisk the eggs, milk, salt and dry mustard in a bowl until blended. Stir in the green chile.

Layer the hash brown potatoes, sausage and cheese in a greased 9×13-inch baking pan. Pour the egg mixture over the prepared layers. Arrange the olives in a decorative pattern over the top. Bake at 350 degrees for 45 to 60 minutes or until set.

Yield: 8 servings

Cinnamon Maple Pears

From Cinnamon Morning Bed & Breakfast

6 pears, peeled, cored, cut into halves
3/4 cup maple syrup

1 teaspoon cinnamon
3 cups whipped cream

Arrange the pear halves cut side up in a shallow baking dish. Drizzle each pear half with 2 tablespoons maple syrup. Sprinkle with the cinnamon. Bake at 350 degrees or microwave until easily pierced with a fork; do not overbake. The pear halves should retain their shape.

Arrange 2 hot pear halves on each of 6 plates. Top with a dollop of whipped cream. Serve immediately.

Yield: 6 servings

Simpático Sides
Vegetables and Side Dishes

The Heart of a Cuisine

New Mexican cuisine is a robust blend of complementary cultures and historical tradition, emerging from an ethnic mix that is at once Native American, Spanish, Mexican, and Anglo. To experience New Mexican foods is to celebrate the centuries: local cooks taking simple and natural ingredients and developing a cuisine unlike any other.

Native Americans who first inhabited New Mexico used indigenous vegetables such as beans, potatoes, corn, and squash and enhanced their flavors with powerful spices such as vanilla and cinnamon.

The Spanish explorer Coronado arrived in 1540 and his presence is evidenced today in our distinctive cuisine, architecture, religions, and arts. The Spaniards introduced new foods to the area such as garlic, onions, wheat, rice, citrus fruits, beef, and pork, as well as the use of lard for frying.

We also can thank the Spaniards for bringing us the chile pepper, that versatile and piquant product that is the principal seasoning of many native dishes. It serves the locals as vegetable, herb, spice, and condiment as well as a lavishly colorful decoration for serene adobe walls, Christmas trees, and so much more.

Just Veggin' Out
Enjoy the Season's Harvest

Vegetable Pancakes

Two-Corn Casserole

Taos Carrot Soufflé

Orange Almond Salad

Serve with a good-quality bottled water garnished with a slice of orange and fresh mint.

Eat Your Vegetables!
Perfect for Those Hot Summer Nights

Portobello Barley Soup

Jicama Salad with Oranges

Creamed Spinach with Cheese

Raspberry Mousse

Serve with raspberry iced tea and French bread.

Río Grande Black Beans

2 cups dried black beans
1 small onion, chopped
1 large garlic clove, minced
1 tablespoon olive oil
1^1/$_2$ teaspoons curry powder
2 bay leaves
1 teaspoon dried oregano
1 teaspoon salt
^{1}/$_2$ teaspoon cumin
^{1}/$_4$ teaspoon pepper
Flour tortillas, heated

Sort and rinse the beans. Combine the beans with a generous amount of water to cover in a bowl. Soak for 8 to 10 hours; do not drain.

Sauté the onion and garlic in the olive oil in a large saucepan. Add the undrained beans, curry powder, bay leaves, oregano, salt, cumin and pepper and mix well. Bring to a boil; reduce heat.

Simmer for 6 to 8 hours or until the beans are tender, stirring occasionally. Discard the bay leaves. Serve with warm flour tortillas. For variety, spoon the beans over hot cooked brown rice or wrap the beans in a flour tortilla with chopped tomatoes, grated carrots and sour cream.

Yield: 4 servings

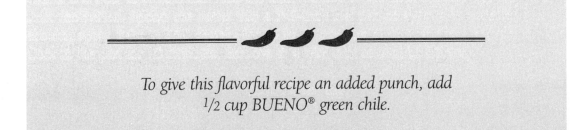

To give this flavorful recipe an added punch, add
1/2 cup BUENO® green chile.

Taos Carrot Soufflé

1 pound carrots, peeled, chopped
1 cup milk
1 cup flour
1 cup sugar
2 eggs
2 teaspoons baking powder
1 teaspoon vanilla extract
1/8 teaspoon salt

Combine the carrots with enough water to cover in a saucepan. Bring to a boil; reduce heat. Cook over medium heat for 20 minutes or until tender; drain. Mash the carrots.

Combine the carrots, milk, flour, sugar, eggs, baking powder, vanilla and salt in a mixing bowl. Beat until smooth, scraping the bowl occasionally. Spoon the carrot mixture into a greased 1¹/₂-quart soufflé dish.

Bake at 350 degrees for 1 hour or until the top is firm to the touch and the edge of the soufflé begins to pull from the side of the dish. Serve immediately.

Yield: 6 to 8 servings

Fresh Corn Bread Pudding

From Seasons Rotisserie & Grill

3/4 cup chopped bacon
1/2 yellow onion, chopped
3 1/2 cups fresh corn kernels
1 3/4 cups heavy cream
3/4 cup chicken stock
1 1/4 cups milk
4 eggs
1 1/2 quarts (1-inch cubes) fresh bread
1 poblano chile, roasted, peeled, chopped
1 cup shredded fontina cheese
Salt and pepper to taste

Fry the bacon in a skillet until crisp. Stir in the onion. Cook until the onion is tender. Add the corn, heavy cream and stock and mix well. Bring to a boil. Cook until the mixture is reduced by half and slightly thickened, stirring frequently. Let stand until cool.

Whisk the milk and eggs in a bowl until blended. Stir in the bread cubes and poblano chile. Add the corn mixture and mix well. Stir in the cheese. Season with salt and pepper.

Spoon the corn mixture into a glass or ceramic baking dish sprayed with nonstick cooking spray. Bake, covered with foil, at 350 degrees for 45 minutes or just until the custard is set in the center; remove cover. Bake for 15 minutes longer or until brown.

Yield: 8 servings

Griddle Corn Cakes

From Doc Martin's Restaurant at The Historic Taos Inn

1³/4 cups flour
2 teaspoons salt
1 teaspoon pepper
2¹/2 cups half-and-half
¹/2 cup (1 stick) butter, melted
2 eggs, lightly beaten
5 cups roasted corn kernels
4 cups julienned zucchini
1 tablespoon chopped shallot

Combine the flour, salt and pepper in a bowl and mix well. Whisk the half-and-half, butter and eggs in a bowl until blended. Add the flour mixture and mix well. Stir in the corn, zucchini and shallot.

Pour enough of the batter onto a hot greased griddle to make a 4-inch circle. Cook until brown on both sides, turning once. Remove to a baking sheet. Keep warm in a 200-degree oven. Repeat the process with the remaining batter.

Yield: 14 corn cakes

Two-Corn Casserole

3/4 cup chopped red bell pepper
1/3 cup chopped onion
1/2 cup (1 stick) butter or margarine
1 (8-ounce) package corn muffin mix
3 eggs, beaten

1 (15-ounce) can cream-style corn
1 (15-ounce) can whole kernel corn
1/2 cup BUENO® frozen green chile
1 cup shredded Cheddar cheese

Sauté the bell pepper and onion in the butter in a skillet until tender-crisp. Combine the muffin mix, eggs, cream-style corn, undrained whole kernel corn and green chile in a bowl and mix well. Add the bell pepper mixture and mix well. Spoon into a greased 2-quart baking dish. Sprinkle with the cheese.

Bake at 350 degrees for 50 to 60 minutes or until set. Let stand for 10 minutes before serving. May be prepared in advance and reheated in the microwave.

Yield: 12 (1/2-cup) servings

Chile Hominy Casserole

2 (20-ounce) cans hominy, drained
1 1/2 cups sour cream
1 1/2 cups shredded Monterey Jack cheese

1/2 cup BUENO® frozen green chile
3 tablespoons grated onion
Salt to taste
1/2 cup fine bread crumbs

Combine the hominy, sour cream, cheese, green chile, onion and salt in a bowl and mix well. Spoon into a baking dish. Sprinkle with the bread crumbs. Bake at 350 degrees for 30 minutes. Add 8 ounces cooked ground chuck, additional grated onion and 1/4 teaspoon garlic powder for a hearty entrée.

Yield: 4 to 6 servings

Leek and Potato Soufflé

From Martin Rios of The Old House

3 russet potatoes, peeled	4 egg yolks
1 leek bulb, thinly sliced	4 egg whites
2 tablespoons butter, melted	1 tablespoon flour

Combine the potatoes with enough water to cover in a saucepan. Cook until tender; drain. Press the potatoes through a potato ricer into a bowl. Let stand until cool. Sauté the leek in the butter in a small sauté pan until tender.

Beat the egg yolks in a mixing bowl until doubled in volume. Beat the egg whites in a mixing bowl until soft peaks form. Fold the egg yolks, egg whites, flour and sautéed leek into the potato purée. Spoon the mixture into four 3-ounce ramekins. Bake at 350 degrees for 8 to 10 minutes or until the volume has increased by 1 1/2 times.

Yield: 4 servings

Green Chile Cheddar Potatoes

From The Bishop's Lodge

2 1/2 pounds potatoes, peeled, coarsely chopped	6 ounces Cheddar cheese, shredded
1/2 cup (1 stick) butter, softened	1/2 cup BUENO® frozen green chile
1/3 cup heavy cream	4 garlic cloves, roasted, minced
2 ounces cream cheese, softened	Salt and pepper to taste

Combine the potatoes with enough water to cover in a large saucepan. Bring to a boil. Boil until tender; drain. Force the potatoes, butter, heavy cream and cream cheese through a food mill into a bowl and mix well. Fold in the Cheddar cheese, green chile and garlic. Season with salt and pepper. Serve immediately.

Yield: 8 servings

Stacked Sicilian Potatoes

8 potatoes, peeled, sliced
Salt to taste
1 tablespoon butter, softened
Milk
2 tablespoons grated Parmesan cheese
Pepper to taste
1 pound bulk Italian sausage, casings removed
8 ounces mozzarella cheese, shredded
Chopped fresh parsley

Combine the potatoes and salt with enough water to cover in a saucepan. Bring to a boil. Boil until tender; drain. Mash the potatoes and butter in a bowl, adding just enough milk as needed for the desired consistency. Stir in the Parmesan cheese. Season with salt and pepper.

Fry the sausage in a skillet, stirring until crumbly; drain. Layer the mozzarella cheese, potatoes and sausage 1/2 at a time in a 5×9-inch loaf pan sprayed with nonstick cooking spray. Sprinkle with parsley. Bake at 400 degrees for 20 minutes or until heated through.

Yield: 8 servings

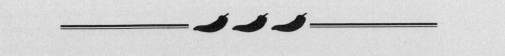

"A unique change from mashed potatoes . . . a Sicilian dish given to me by my grandmother who arrived in this country in 1907."

Creamed Spinach with Cheese

2 (10-ounce) packages frozen chopped spinach
1/4 cup (1/2 stick) butter
2 tablespoons flour
2 tablespoons chopped onion
1/2 cup evaporated milk
6 ounces Pepper Jack cheese, cubed
1 teaspoon Worcestershire sauce
3/4 teaspoon celery salt
3/4 teaspoon garlic salt
1/2 teaspoon black pepper
Red pepper to taste

Cook the spinach using package directions. Drain, reserving 1/2 cup of the liquid. Heat the butter in a saucepan over low heat until melted. Stir in the flour. Cook until blended, stirring constantly. Add the onion and mix well.

Cook until the onion is tender but not brown, stirring frequently. Add the reserved spinach liquid and evaporated milk gradually, stirring constantly. Cook until thickened, stirring constantly. Stir in the cheese, Worcestershire sauce, celery salt, garlic salt, black pepper and red pepper.

Cook until the cheese melts, stirring constantly. Add the spinach and mix well. Serve immediately or spoon the spinach mixture into a 2-quart baking dish and sprinkle with buttered bread crumbs. Chill, covered, for 8 to 10 hours. Bake at 350 degrees for 20 to 25 minutes or until heated through. You may freeze for future use.

Yield: 6 to 8 servings

Butternut Squash with Maple Syrup

3/4 cup pure maple syrup
1/2 cup (1 stick) butter
1/4 cup apple juice
2 teaspoons cinnamon
1 teaspoon allspice
3/4 teaspoon salt
3 small butternut squash, peeled, cut into halves lengthwise,
cut into 1/3-inch slices crosswise
4 (6-ounce) Granny Smith apples, peeled, cut into halves,
cut into 1/4-inch slices
Salt and pepper to taste

Combine the maple syrup, butter and apple juice in a saucepan. Cook over medium-low heat until the butter melts, stirring occasionally. Increase the heat to high. Bring to a boil. Boil for 5 minutes or until the mixture is slightly reduced, stirring frequently. Remove from heat. Whisk in the cinnamon, allspice and 3/4 teaspoon salt.

Arrange 1/3 of the squash in a buttered 9×13-inch baking dish. Top with 1/2 of the apples slices and 1/2 of the remaining squash. Arrange the remaining squash and apple slices slightly overlapping over the top. Sprinkle lightly with salt and pepper to taste. Pour the maple syrup mixture over the prepared layers.

Bake, covered with foil, at 400 degrees for 50 minutes or until the squash is almost tender. Remove the cover. Bake for 20 minutes longer or until the squash is tender, basting occasionally with the syrup mixture. Spoon the syrup mixture over the vegetables and serve immediately. You may bake 1 day in advance and store, covered, in the refrigerator. Reheat at 350 degrees for 25 minutes or microwave on High for 8 minutes.

Yield: 8 to 10 servings

Sweet Potato and Banana Bake

6 medium bananas, cut into ¹/2-inch slices
¹/4 cup orange juice
1 teaspoon vanilla extract
¹/2 cup packed light brown sugar
¹/2 teaspoon cinnamon
4 pounds sweet potatoes, peeled, cooked, cut into ¹/2-inch slices
2 tablespoons butter or margarine, coarsely chopped

Toss the bananas, orange juice and vanilla gently in a bowl. Combine the brown sugar and cinnamon in a bowl and mix well. Drain the bananas, reserving the orange juice mixture. Arrange ¹/3 of the sweet potato slices slightly overlapping in a greased 2-quart soufflé or deep baking dish. Layer with ¹/2 of the banana slices, ¹/3 of the brown sugar mixture and ¹/3 of the butter. Reserve some of the remaining banana slices for the top.

Layer ¹/2 of the remaining potatoes, remaining bananas, ¹/2 of the brown sugar mixture and ¹/2 of the butter over the prepared layers. Repeat the layers with the remaining ingredients. Drizzle with the reserved orange juice mixture. Top with the reserved bananas. Bake at 375 degrees for 45 minutes or until bubbly.

Yield: 12 servings

Zucchini Julienne

1 medium red bell pepper, cut into 2-inch strips
¹/2 large yellow onion, julienned
1 tablespoon unsalted butter
1 tablespoon olive oil
5 small zucchini, cut into 2-inch strips
Salt and pepper to taste
Garlic powder to taste
2 tablespoons grated Parmesan cheese

Cook the bell pepper and onion in the butter and olive oil in a 12-inch nonstick skillet over medium heat until the vegetables are slightly softened. Stir in the zucchini, salt, pepper and garlic powder. Cook for 5 minutes or until the vegetables are tender-crisp, stirring frequently. Spoon into a serving bowl. Sprinkle with the cheese.

Yield: 6 servings

Vegetable Pancakes

Pancakes

1 cup finely chopped red bell pepper
1 large carrot, finely chopped
1/3 cup chicken broth
1/2 cup frozen corn kernels, thawed
1/2 teaspoon dried oregano
1/4 teaspoon salt
1 cup ricotta cheese
1 cup cottage cheese
1/2 cup flour
1/2 teaspoon baking powder
3 egg whites, lightly beaten
1/4 teaspoon salt
1 tablespoon vegetable oil

Red Pepper and Corn Relish

1 cup finely chopped red bell pepper
1/2 cup frozen corn kernels, thawed
2 scallions, thinly sliced
1 tablespoon lime juice
2 teaspoons chopped fresh parsley
1 teaspoon honey
1/4 teaspoon salt

For the pancakes, combine the bell pepper, carrot and broth in a saucepan. Bring to a boil. Boil for 5 minutes or until the bell pepper is tender. Stir in the corn, oregano and 1/4 teaspoon salt. Cook for 2 to 3 minutes longer, stirring occasionally. Let stand until cool. Stir in the ricotta cheese, cottage cheese, flour, baking powder, egg whites, and 1/4 teaspoon salt. Heat the oil in a large nonstick skillet until hot. Drop the batter by 1/3 cupfuls into the hot skillet. Cook for 2 minutes per side or until brown, turning once. Transfer the pancakes to a baking sheet. Keep warm in a 250-degree oven.

For the relish, combine the bell pepper, corn, scallions, lime juice, parsley, honey and salt in a bowl and mix well. Top each pancake with some of the relish.

Yield: 20 (4-inch) pancakes

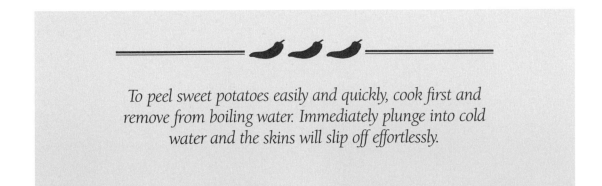

To peel sweet potatoes easily and quickly, cook first and remove from boiling water. Immediately plunge into cold water and the skins will slip off effortlessly.

Polenta with Parmesan

8 ounces cornmeal
3 cups heavy cream
3 cups water
1 cup grated Parmesan cheese
1 tablespoon salt

Combine the cornmeal, heavy cream and water in a saucepan and mix well. Cook over medium heat until slightly thickened, stirring frequently. Reduce the heat. Cook for 15 minutes longer, stirring constantly. Remove from heat. Stir in the Parmesan cheese and salt. Cook for 2 minutes longer, stirring constantly.

Yield: 4 servings

Kiva Rice

1 pound Monterey Jack cheese, shredded
2 cups uncooked rice
2 cups sour cream
1 cup BUENO® frozen green chile, drained
1 cup water

Combine the cheese, rice, sour cream, green chile and water in a bowl and mix well. Spoon into a 9×13-inch baking dish.

Bake, covered with foil, at 350 degrees for 40 minutes. Remove the cover. Bake for 5 minutes longer.

Yield: 6 servings

Lemon Piñon Rice

From Casa del Granjero "The Farmer's House" Bed & Breakfast

1/2 cup piñons (pine nuts)
1/2 cup (1 stick) butter
1/2 cup finely chopped red bell pepper
1/4 cup finely chopped green bell pepper
4 scallions, minced

1 tablespoon minced garlic
1 1/2 cups cooked white rice
1/2 cup fresh lemon juice
1/2 cup minced fresh parsley
1 lemon, cut into wedges
6 sprigs of parsley

Sauté the piñons in the butter in a skillet for 3 minutes. Stir in the bell peppers, scallions and garlic. Sauté for 5 minutes. Stir in the rice. Cook just until heated through, stirring constantly. Add the lemon juice and minced parsley and mix well. Spoon into a serving bowl. Top with the lemon wedges and parsley sprigs.

Yield: 6 servings

Lemony Pine Nut Pilaf

2 cups chicken broth
1 cup white rice
2 1/2 tablespoons butter or margarine
1/2 cup pine nuts or sunflower kernels

3 tablespoons chopped fresh parsley
2 tablespoons lemon juice
1 tablespoon grated lemon zest

Bring the broth to a boil in a saucepan. Stir in the rice. Simmer, covered, for 20 to 25 minutes or until the rice is tender and the broth has been absorbed.

Heat the butter in a saucepan until melted. Stir in the pine nuts. Cook until golden brown, stirring constantly. Stir in the parsley, lemon juice and lemon zest. Pour over the rice and toss to coat. Serve immediately.

Yield: 6 servings

Wild Rice with Cherries and Apricots

18 ounces pearl onions
2 tablespoons butter
4 1/2 cups reduced-sodium chicken broth
1 tablespoon chopped fresh thyme
1 1/4 cups wild rice, rinsed, drained
1 1/4 cups long grain white rice
1 (6-ounce) package dried apricots, coarsely chopped
1 cup dried tart cherries or cranberries
1 cup raisins
2 tablespoons chopped fresh thyme
1/4 cup (1/2 stick) butter
1 cup pecans, toasted, chopped
Salt and pepper to taste
1/2 cup dried tart cherries or cranberries

Blanch the onions in boiling water in a saucepan for 1 minute. Drain and peel. Sauté the onions in 2 tablespoons butter in a large skillet over medium heat for 15 minutes or until brown.

Bring the broth and 1 tablespoon thyme to a boil in a saucepan. Stir in the wild rice. Bring to a boil; reduce heat. Simmer, covered, for 30 minutes. Stir in the white rice. Simmer, covered, for 15 minutes or until the rice is tender and the liquid has been absorbed. Stir in the apricots, 1 cup cherries, raisins and 2 tablespoons thyme. Simmer, covered, for 3 minutes. Stir in the onions and 1/4 cup butter. Add the pecans and mix well. Season with salt and pepper.

Spoon the rice mixture into a buttered 9×13-inch baking dish. Coat 1 side of a sheet of foil with butter and place the foil butter side down over the rice mixture. Bake at 350 degrees for 25 minutes; remove the cover. Sprinkle with 1/2 cup cherries. Bake for 5 minutes longer or until heated through.

Yield: 8 to 10 servings

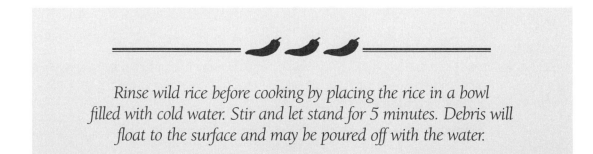

Rinse wild rice before cooking by placing the rice in a bowl filled with cold water. Stir and let stand for 5 minutes. Debris will float to the surface and may be poured off with the water.

Raisin and Walnut Kugel

16 ounces medium egg noodles
Salt to taste
6 medium eggs
1$1/2$ cups milk
1 cup cottage cheese
1 cup sour cream
1 cup raisins
$1/2$ cup sugar
$1/2$ cup packed brown sugar
$1/2$ cup chopped walnuts
1 tablespoon cinnamon

Cook the noodles in lightly salted boiling water in a saucepan until tender; drain. Whisk the eggs in a bowl until blended. Stir in the milk, cottage cheese, sour cream, raisins and sugar. Fold in the noodles. Spoon the noodle mixture into a buttered 10×14-inch baking dish.

Combine the brown sugar, walnuts and cinnamon in a bowl and mix well. Sprinkle over the prepared layer. Bake at 350 degrees for 1 hour or until the center is firm. Cool slightly. Serve warm or at room temperature.

Yield: 10 servings

Comidas by Candlelight
Entrées

The Portal of Accord

Occupying the north side of the plaza in Santa Fe, the Palace of the Governors and its Museum of New Mexico has been a center of activity since Santa Fe's founding in 1610. For decades, the museum has worked to preserve and promote Native American arts and crafts. The portal, or front porch, of the Palace of the Governors is reserved for authorized participants representing all ninteen New Mexican pueblos. Having put aside past conflicts and contemporary tensions, the portal provides an excellent example in multicultural collaboration.

Technical mastery of their arts and crafts skills is required of participants in the Native American Vendors Program. All work is carefully monitored and inspected by ten program participants plus the portal committee, which is elected annually by their peers.

There are no assigned locations under the portal. The system for assigning spaces was devised by the vendors and is elegant in its simplicity. The sixty-nine available spaces are claimed at 8 A.M. daily on a first-come, first-served basis. If there are more than sixty-nine vendors, a lottery is held by putting numbered chips and additional blank chips to correspond with the vendor count. Participants then draw chips to select the allotted spaces. Fifty-nine of these spaces may also be shared, resulting in actual capacity of over one hundred vendors.

The Palace Portal attracts over two million visitors annually and provides an incomparable opportunity to talk to Native Americans in an historically significant setting.

Dinner with a Flair

For Special People—Such as Yourself

Crab Cakes with Chipotle Aïoli

Marinated Asparagus

Leg of Lamb with Artichokes

Lemon Piñon Rice

Coconut Sour Cream Cake

Serve with your favorite chardonnay or red wine

such as a Merlot or zinfandel.

Unexpected Elegance

For Those Last-Minute Dinner Guests

Sun-Dried Tomato Mousse

Far East Spinach Salad

Jalapeño Orange Shrimp and Pasta

Gingersnap Pie

Grab a loaf of French bread and toast it with butter and a little garlic.

Green Chile Brisket

From Tinnie Mercantile Store & Deli

6 medium onions
1 (56-ounce) tub frozen BUENO® mild green chile, thawed
1/3 cup dried oregano
1/3 cup cumin
1/4 cup granulated garlic
1 (12- to 15-pound) beef brisket, trimmed
Salt and pepper to taste

Process the onions, green chile, oregano, cumin and garlic in a food processor until of a pasty consistency. Sprinkle the surface of the brisket with salt and pepper. Coat with the green chile paste. Wrap the brisket in heavy-duty foil.

Place the brisket in a deep baking pan. Add enough water to cover the brisket. Bake at 225 degrees for 12 hours or longer, adding additional water as needed. Drain the liquid from the brisket, reserving the chile mixture. The brisket should be so tender it falls apart.

Pour the drained chile mixture over the brisket and chop. Serve on buns for a great sandwich or as an entrée.

Yield: 20 servings

Marinated Flank Steak with Horseradish Sauce

Horseradish Sauce
1/2 cup sour cream
1 tablespoon plus 1 teaspoon finely chopped horseradish
2 green onions, finely chopped

Steak
1/2 cup soy sauce
1/2 cup white wine
1/2 cup chopped onion
3 tablespoons chopped fresh rosemary
2 tablespoons olive oil
2 garlic cloves, chopped
2 pounds flank steak

For the sauce, combine the sour cream, horseradish and green onions in a bowl and mix well. Chill, covered, until serving time.

For the steak, combine the soy sauce, wine, onion, rosemary, olive oil and garlic in a bowl and mix well. Pour over the steak in a shallow dish, turning to coat. Marinate, covered, in the refrigerator for 8 to 10 hours, turning occasionally.

Drain the steak, reserving the marinade. Grill the steak over hot coals for 6 minutes per side for rare, basting occasionally if desired with the reserved marinade. Remove the steak to a serving platter. Let stand for 15 minutes. Slice as desired and serve with the horseradish sauce.

Yield: 6 to 8 servings

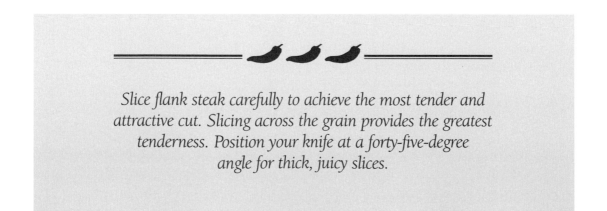

Slice flank steak carefully to achieve the most tender and attractive cut. Slicing across the grain provides the greatest tenderness. Position your knife at a forty-five-degree angle for thick, juicy slices.

Peppered Seared Porter Steaks

From The Ranchers Club

3 shallots, chopped	6 leeks
1 carrot, sliced	1 cup chopped fresh Italian
2 tablespoons vegetable oil	parsley
8 button mushrooms	1 cup chicken stock
8 peppercorns	1 cup chopped onion
1 tablespoon honey	5 tablespoons butter
2 cups porter or dark beer	1 teaspoon thyme
8 cups veal stock	1 tablespoon vegetable oil
Salt and pepper to taste	6 sirloin strip steaks

Sauté the shallots and carrot in 2 tablespoons oil in a saucepan over medium heat. Add the mushrooms and peppercorns gradually, stirring constantly. Sauté for 6 minutes or until caramelized. Stir in the honey.

Cook for 3 minutes, stirring frequently. Add the beer and mix well. Cook until reduced by 2/3, stirring frequently. Stir in the veal stock. Simmer for 2 hours or until the mixture is reduced to 2/3 cup, stirring occasionally. Strain through a sieve into a bowl, discarding the solids. Season with salt and pepper. Return the sauce to the saucepan. Cover to keep warm.

Julienne the leeks and rinse under cold water. Bring the leeks, parsley, chicken stock, onion, butter, thyme, salt and pepper to a simmer in a saucepan, stirring occasionally. Simmer until the leeks are tender, stirring occasionally. Remove from heat. Drain, reserving the leeks. Cover to keep warm.

Heat 1 tablespoon oil in a skillet over medium heat. Add the steaks. Sauté until of the desired degree of doneness, turning once or twice. Arrange the steaks on 6 dinner plates. Top each steak with leeks and drizzle with the desired amount of the beer sauce.

Yield: 6 servings

Steak Dunigan

From The Pink Adobe

Pink Adobe Green Chile Sauce
1 medium onion, finely chopped
2 tablespoons olive oil
1 cup BUENO® frozen green chile, drained
1 teaspoon Tabasco sauce or chopped jalapeño chile
1/4 teaspoon dried oregano
1/4 teaspoon minced fresh cilantro
1/4 teaspoon salt

Steaks
4 large mushrooms, thinly sliced
1/4 cup (1/2 stick) butter
Hickory-smoked salt to taste
2 (14- to 15-ounce) New York-cut sirloin steaks

For the sauce, sauté the onion in the olive oil in an ovenproof saucepan. Stir in the green chile, Tabasco sauce, oregano, cilantro and salt. Cook for 5 minutes, stirring occasionally. Keep warm in a 200-degree oven.

For the steaks, sauté the mushrooms in the butter in an ovenproof saucepan for 5 minutes or until tender. Keep warm in a 200-degree oven. Sprinkle the hickory-smoked salt over the surface of the steaks. Broil or grill over hot coals for 10 to 15 minutes for rare or 15 to 20 minutes for medium, turning once. Transfer the steaks to a serving platter. Top each steak with an equal portion of the mushrooms. Spread with the sauce.

Yield: 2 servings

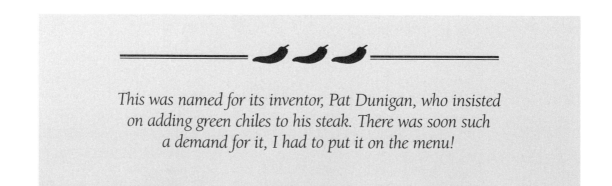

This was named for its inventor, Pat Dunigan, who insisted on adding green chiles to his steak. There was soon such a demand for it, I had to put it on the menu!

Tequila-Marinated Fajitas

1/2 (one-fifth) tequila
1 cup olive oil
2 limes, cut into halves
2 oranges, cut into halves
2 lemons, cut into halves
1/4 cup BUENO®
crushed red chile
2 tablespoons kosher salt
2 tablespoons dried oregano
1 tablespoon crushed
black pepper

5 pounds sirloin steak,
thinly sliced
3 bell peppers, julienned
3 yellow onions, julienned
6 jalapeño chiles, julienned
20 BUENO® flour tortillas,
heated
Guacamole
Sour cream
Salsa

Combine the tequila, olive oil, limes, oranges, lemons, red chile, kosher salt, oregano and black pepper in a large bowl and mix well. Add the steak and toss to coat. Marinate, covered, in the refrigerator for 8 hours, stirring occasionally. Drain the steak, discarding the marinade. Sear the steak in a hot skillet until light brown. Add the bell peppers, onions and jalapeño chiles. Cook until the vegetables are tender, stirring frequently. Serve in the warm tortillas topped with guacamole, sour cream and/or salsa.

Yield: 20 fajitas

Marinades can add layers of complexity to a dish with very little effort. Because of their acidic nature, they are wonderful for tenderizing meat or permeating a piece of fish with an exciting and unexpected flavor. On pages 154 and 155 are some of our favorite marinades that are great with both meat and fish.

Almond Chicken in Green Sauce

From Jane Butel

1 (3-pound) chicken, cut up
2 cups (about) chicken broth
2 tablespoons pickled jalapeño chile juice
1 large onion, cut into quarters
6 to 8 dark green lettuce leaves (romaine, leaf lettuce or outer leaves of iceberg lettuce)
1 cup Italian parsley sprigs

$^1/_2$ cup fresh cilantro leaves
6 fresh or pickled jalapeño chiles, stems removed
1 large garlic clove
2 tablespoons virgin olive oil
1 cup ground almonds
Salt to taste
12 corn tortillas, heated, or 3 to 4 cups hot cooked rice
Guacamole (optional)
2 cups sour cream (optional)

Arrange the chicken in a single layer in a stockpot. Pour the broth and jalapeño chile juice over the chicken. Bring to a boil; reduce heat. Simmer, covered, for 35 to 45 minutes or just until tender. Let stand in broth until cool. Remove the chicken to a platter with a slotted spoon, reserving the broth. Chop the chicken into bite-size pieces, discarding the skin and bones.

Process the onion, lettuce leaves, parsley, cilantro leaves, jalapeño chiles and garlic in a food processor until smooth. Add approximately 1 cup of the reserved broth 1 tablespoon at a time, processing constantly until the mixture is of the consistency of whipping cream.

Heat the olive oil in a heavy saucepan until hot. Stir in the almonds. Cook over medium-low heat for 3 to 5 minutes or just until lightly toasted. Stir in the green sauce and chicken. Simmer for 10 to 15 minutes or until the flavors are blended and the mixture is heated through, stirring occasionally. Taste and adjust seasonings, adding salt if desired. Serve in warm tortillas or over rice topped with guacamole and sour cream.

For a slightly lower fat and calorie version, reduce the olive oil to 1 tablespoon and the almonds to $^2/_3$ cup.

Yield: 6 servings

Chicken Mesilla

From Double Eagle Restaurant

1 yellow onion, thinly sliced
1 tablespoon butter
1 garlic clove, minced
4 boneless skinless chicken breasts
Salt and pepper to taste
Olive oil (optional)
4 whole BUENO® frozen green chiles, roasted
1¹/3 cups shredded Monterey Jack cheese

Combine the onion and butter in a sauté pan. Cook over medium heat until caramelized. Do not stir until the onions turn golden brown and then stir just to turn. Stir in the garlic. Remove from heat. Spoon the caramelized onions into 4 equal mounds in a shallow baking dish.

Sprinkle the chicken with salt and pepper. Cook the chicken in the sauté pan over medium heat until cooked through, turning once and adding olive oil as needed. Arrange a chicken breast over each onion mound. Top each with 1 green chile and ¹/3 cup cheese. Bake at 325 degrees for 6 to 8 minutes or until the cheese melts.

Yield: 4 servings

The Double Eagle restaurant building, listed on the National Historic Register and over 150 years old, is filled with antiques, museum quality paintings, sculptures, and huge crystal chandeliers. Stories of encounters with two ghostly lovers who died in the home in 1849 abound. The restaurant features steaks and seafood and a surprise . . . a separate café within the restaurant offering New Mexican-style foods such as shark fajitas and banana enchiladas.

Grilled Chicken with Black Bean Salsa

Black Bean Salsa

1 (15-ounce) can black beans, drained, rinsed
1 1/2 cups frozen corn, thawed
1 cup chopped tomato
1/2 cup chopped red onion (optional)
1/4 cup finely chopped cilantro
1 jalapeño chile, finely chopped
1/2 cup balsamic vinegar
1/4 cup vegetable oil
1 1/2 tablespoons Dijon mustard
1/4 teaspoon salt
1/4 teaspoon pepper

Chicken

6 boneless skinless chicken breasts
Salt and pepper to taste

For the salsa, combine the beans, corn, tomato, onion, cilantro and jalapeño chile in a bowl and mix well. Whisk the balsamic vinegar, oil, Dijon mustard, salt and pepper in a bowl. Pour the vinegar mixture over the bean mixture and toss to coat. Marinate at room temperature for 2 hours or longer, stirring occasionally.

For the chicken, sprinkle both sides of the chicken with salt and pepper. Grill over hot coals until cooked through, turning once. Serve with the salsa.

Yield: 6 servings

Taos, New Mexico, is actually made up of three villages. Taos proper, legally Don Fernando de Taos, is the original Spanish town, which is now a center of art and tourism. Pueblo de Taos, San Geronimo de Taos, is home of the conservative Taos Indians and remains much as it was before the Spanish conquest. Ranchos de Taos is the farming community whose mission church is one of the most frequently depicted structures in the state.

Chicken Fajitas

1/2 cup tomato juice
1/2 cup lime juice
1/2 cup soy sauce
1/2 cup packed brown sugar
3 tablespoons vegetable oil
3 garlic cloves, minced
1 teaspoon pepper
1 1/2 pounds chicken pieces
1 1/2 cups sliced onions
1 1/2 cups sliced green or red bell peppers
2 tablespoons vegetable oil
6 BUENO® flour tortillas
2 cups shredded lettuce
1 1/2 cups chopped tomatoes
1 cup shredded cheese
1 cup sour cream
1 cup salsa

Combine the tomato juice, lime juice, soy sauce, brown sugar, 3 tablespoons oil, garlic and pepper in a bowl and mix well. Pour over the chicken in a shallow dish, turning to coat. Marinate in the refrigerator for 2 to 4 hours, turning occasionally; drain.

Brush the chicken, onions and bell peppers with 2 tablespoons oil. Grill the chicken over hot coals for 5 minutes or until cooked through, turning once. Grill the vegetables until tender-crisp, turning occasionally. Microwave the tortillas for 30 seconds or just until warm. Shred the chicken, discarding the skin and bones.

Arrange the chicken, onions and bell peppers on a serving platter. Serve with the tortillas, lettuce, tomatoes, cheese, sour cream and salsa.

Yield: 6 servings

Chicken Shortcake Pie

From The Albuquerque Petroleum Club

Crust

3/4 cup flour
1 teaspoon dried basil, crushed
1/4 cup (1/2 stick) butter or margarine
2 tablespoons milk

Filling

2 (8-ounce) chicken breasts, boned, skinned, cut into strips
2 tablespoons flour
1/2 cup chopped red bell pepper
1/3 cup chopped onion
1/3 cup chopped celery
3 tablespoons butter or margarine
1 1/2 ounces cream cheese, cubed
1/4 cup milk
1/4 cup sour cream
1/8 teaspoon pepper

Topping

1/4 cup dry seasoned bread crumbs
1 tablespoon grated Parmesan cheese
1 tablespoon butter or margarine, melted
Red bell pepper strips
Celery leaves

For the crust, combine the flour and basil in a bowl and mix well. Cut in the butter until crumbly. Add the milk, stirring just until moistened. Pat the dough over the bottom and up the side of a 9-inch glass pie plate. Bake at 350 degrees for 12 minutes.

For the filling, coat the chicken with the flour. Sauté the bell pepper, onion and celery in the butter in a skillet until tender but not brown. Add the chicken. Cook for 2 to 3 minutes longer or until the chicken is cooked through, stirring frequently. Stir in the cream cheese, milk, sour cream and pepper. Spoon the chicken mixture into the baked crust. Bake at 350 degrees for 15 minutes or until heated through.

For the topping, combine the bread crumbs, cheese and butter in a bowl and mix well. Sprinkle the crumb mixture over the top of the baked layers. Bake for 5 minutes longer. Top with bell pepper strips and celery leaves.

Yield: 4 servings

Pan-Roasted Duck Breast

From Martin Rios of The Old House

Huckleberry Ancho Chile Sauce

1 cup canned chicken broth
1 small onion, chopped
1 cup apple juice
1/2 cup cassis purée

2 ancho chiles, seeded
1 cup frozen or canned
huckleberries or blueberries
Salt and pepper to taste

Duck and Assembly

1/4 cup vegetable oil
4 (4- to 5-ounce)
  duck breasts

Leek and Potato Soufflé
(page 112)

For the sauce, combine the broth, onion, apple juice, cassis purée and ancho chiles in a saucepan. Bring to a boil. Boil until reduced by 1/2, stirring frequently. Transfer the mixture to a blender container. Process until puréed. Press the purée through a sieve into the saucepan, discarding the solids. Stir in the huckleberries. Season with salt and pepper. Simmer just until heated through, stirring frequently. Remove from heat. Cover to keep warm.

For the duck, heat the oil in a medium sauté pan. Arrange the duck breast side down in the hot oil. Cook over medium heat until the skin is crispy; turn. Cook for 5 minutes longer or until the duck is cooked through. Let rest for 1 to 2 minutes. Slice as desired.

To assemble, spoon some of the Leek and Potato Soufflé in the center of each of 4 dinner plates. Arrange 1 sliced duck breast over the soufflé. Drizzle the sauce around the soufflé and duck.

Yield: 4 servings

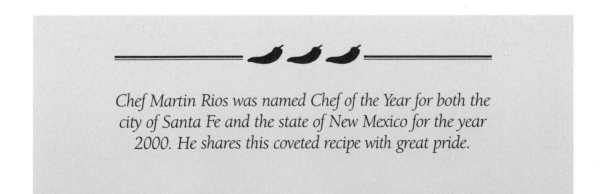

Chef Martin Rios was named Chef of the Year for both the city of Santa Fe and the state of New Mexico for the year 2000. He shares this coveted recipe with great pride.

Quick Tamale Casserole
Cacerola de Tamales

From PNM's Cocinas de New Mexico

1 pound ground beef
4 ounces ground pork
1/2 cup chopped onion
1 garlic clove, minced
2 cups canned tomatoes
1/2 cup chopped black olives
2 tablespoons BUENO® frozen green chile
1 teaspoon salt
1/8 teaspoon pepper
1/4 cup shredded sharp Cheddar cheese
2 tablespoons cornmeal
3 cups water
1 cup cornmeal
1 1/2 cups shredded sharp Cheddar cheese

Brown the ground beef and ground pork in a skillet over medium heat, stirring until crumbly. Stir in the onion and garlic. Cook until the onion is tender, stirring constantly; drain. Add the tomatoes, olives, green chile, salt and pepper and mix well.

Cook for 20 minutes, stirring occasionally and adding water as desired for a thinner consistency. Stir in 1/4 cup cheese and 2 tablespoons cornmeal. Cook for 2 to 3 minutes, stirring frequently. Remove from heat.

Combine 3 cups water and 1 cup cornmeal in a saucepan and mix well. Cook until thickened, stirring frequently. Spread half the cornmeal mixture in a greased 9×13-inch baking pan. Spread with the ground beef mixture. Top with the remaining cornmeal mixture. Sprinkle with 1 1/2 cups cheese. Bake at 350 degrees for 20 minutes.

Yield: 12 servings

Leg of Lamb with Artichokes

1 leg of lamb, boned
1 garlic clove
Salt and pepper to taste
1/3 cup chopped onion
3 tablespoons butter
1/2 cup coarsely chopped canned or frozen artichoke hearts
1 cup fresh bread crumbs
2 teaspoons chopped fresh parsley
1/4 teaspoon salt
1/8 teaspoon dried thyme
1/8 teaspoon dried marjoram
1/8 teaspoon dried dillweed
1/8 teaspoon pepper
1 1/2 cups beef consommé
2 teaspoons flour

Rub the inside and outside of the lamb with the garlic clove. Sprinkle with salt and pepper. Sauté the onion in the butter in a skillet until golden brown. Stir in the artichokes. Cook for 1 minute, stirring frequently. Add the bread crumbs, parsley, 1/4 teaspoon salt, thyme, marjoram, dillweed and 1/8 teaspoon pepper and mix well. Spoon the stuffing inside the lamb. Secure with skewers and kitchen twine.

Arrange the lamb on a rack in a roasting pan. Bake at 325 degrees for 43 minutes per pound for medium-rare, basting with 1/2 cup of the consommé 20 minutes before the end of the baking process. Remove the lamb to a heated platter.

Drain the pan drippings, reserving 2 tablespoons. Combine the reserved 2 tablespoons pan drippings and flour in the roasting pan and mix until blended. Add the remaining 1 cup consommé, stirring constantly until smooth. Cook until thickened, stirring constantly. Season with salt and pepper. Serve with the lamb.

Yield: 4 to 6 servings

Río Grande Pork Roast
Puerco Asado del Río Grande

From PNM's Cocinas de New Mexico

1 (3- to 4-pound) boneless pork roast
1/2 teaspoon BUENO® chile powder
1/2 teaspoon garlic powder
1/2 teaspoon salt

1 cup apple jelly
1 cup ketchup
1 tablespoon vinegar
2 teaspoons BUENO® chile powder
1 1/2 cups crushed corn chips

Rub the surface of the pork with a mixture of 1/2 teaspoon chile powder, garlic powder and salt. Arrange the pork in a roasting pan. Roast at 325 degrees for 1 hour.

Combine the apple jelly, ketchup, vinegar and 2 teaspoons chile powder in a saucepan. Simmer over low heat for 15 minutes, stirring occasionally. Baste the roast with half the sauce and top with half the corn chips. Roast for 35 to 40 minutes per pound or until cooked through. Remove the pork to a serving platter.

Bring the remaining sauce to a boil. Boil for 2 minutes, stirring occasionally. Serve the sauce and remaining corn chips with the pork.

Yield: 8 to 10 servings

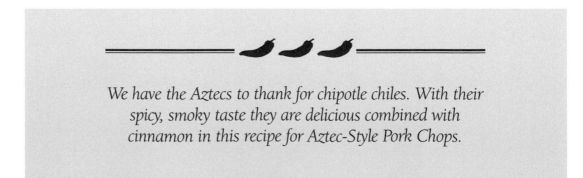

We have the Aztecs to thank for chipotle chiles. With their spicy, smoky taste they are delicious combined with cinnamon in this recipe for Aztec-Style Pork Chops.

Aztec-Style Pork Chops

From Jane Butel

2 dried chipotle chiles
1/2 cup hot water
4 garlic cloves, minced
1 tablespoon ground mild red chile
1/4 cup honey

1 1/2 teaspoons ground cinnamon
4 pork loin chops, 1 inch thick, trimmed
4 (1/4-inch-thick) slices jicama
4 cinnamon sticks

Combine the chipotle chiles and hot water in a small bowl. Let stand for 10 minutes. Drain, reserving the liquid. Chop the chiles. Combine the chiles with the next 4 ingredients in a bowl and mix well. Add just enough of the reserved liquid until of the consistency of a thick paste and mix well. Marinate the pork chops in the sauce in a shallow dish for 10 to 15 minutes; drain. Grill the pork chops over hot coals for 8 minutes per side. Grill the jicama until light brown on both sides. Top each pork chop with a cinnamon stick and grilled jicama slice.

Yield: 4 servings

Asian Baby Back Ribs

4 to 5 pounds baby back pork ribs
1 1/2 cups ketchup
1 1/2 cups soy sauce
1/2 cup honey
1/3 cup dry sherry

3 tablespoons minced gingerroot
1 tablespoon chopped fresh rosemary (optional)
1 tablespoon minced garlic
2 tablespoons chopped scallions

Arrange the ribs in a large shallow dish. Combine the next 7 ingredients in a bowl and mix well. Pour over the ribs, turning to coat. Marinate, loosely covered, in the refrigerator for 8 to 10 hours, turning occasionally. Arrange the ribs on a rack in a roasting pan. Pour the marinade over the ribs. Bake at 400 degrees for 1 1/4 hours, basting frequently. Sprinkle with the scallions before serving.

Yield: 4 to 6 servings

Glazed Baby Back Ribs with Guajillo Barbecue Sauce

From Coyote Café

Ribs

1 1/2 cups apple cider vinegar
1 cup balsamic vinegar
1 cup honey
6 tablespoons honey mustard
1/4 cup liquid smoke
2 tablespoons chopped fresh thyme

2 tablespoons chile molido
2 tablespoons freshly ground pepper
1 tablespoon coriander
1 tablespoon salt
2 racks baby back pork ribs
(3 1/2 to 4 pounds)

Guajillo Barbecue Sauce

1 cup chopped white onion
1 1/2 teaspoons minced garlic
1 tablespoon unsalted butter
1/4 cup sherry vinegar
3 whole guajillo chiles, stems removed, crushed

1 1/4 cups tomato purée
1 cup strong black coffee
1/3 cup molasses
1 teaspoon freshly ground pepper
1/2 teaspoon salt

For the ribs, combine the cider vinegar, balsamic vinegar, honey, honey mustard, liquid smoke, thyme, chile molido, pepper, coriander and salt in a bowl and mix well. Arrange the ribs in a nonreactive dish. Pour the marinade over the ribs, turning to coat. Marinate, covered, in the refrigerator for 8 to 10 hours, turning occasionally. Drain the ribs, reserving the marinade. Strain the reserved marinade into a bowl. Wrap the ribs in foil and place on baking sheets. Bake at 225 degrees for 2 hours or until tender.

For the sauce, cook the onion and garlic in the butter in a sauté pan over low heat for 10 minutes, stirring frequently. Deglaze the pan with the sherry vinegar. Stir in the guajillo chiles, tomato purée, coffee, molasses, pepper and salt. Simmer over low heat until the guajillo chiles are tender, stirring occasionally. Process the sauce in a blender until smooth. Strain through a sieve into a bowl. You may store the sauce, covered, in the refrigerator for up to 2 weeks. Remove the ribs from the foil. Grill if desired over hot coals for a smokier flavor and crusty texture, basting with the reserved marinade 2 to 3 times. Slice the ribs into serving portions and serve with the sauce.

Yield: 4 to 6 servings

Crab Cakes with Chipotle Aïoli

From Seasons Rotisserie & Grill

Chipotle Aïoli

2 egg yolks	2 canned chipotle chiles
Juice of 1/2 lemon	in adobo
2 teaspoons minced garlic	1 1/2 cups olive oil
1 teaspoon adobo sauce	Salt and white pepper to taste

Crab Cakes

1/2 red bell pepper, finely chopped	1 1/2 cups bread crumbs
	3 eggs, lightly beaten
1/2 yellow bell pepper, finely chopped	1 egg yolk, lightly beaten
	1 tablespoon chopped fresh parsley
2 ribs celery, finely chopped	1 tablespoon chopped fresh basil
1 shallot, minced	1/8 teaspoon cayenne pepper
1 tablespoon olive oil	Salt and pepper to taste
1 1/4 pounds blue crab meat, drained	1 cup bread crumbs
	2 tablespoons canola oil
1 1/4 pounds Canadian snow crab meat, drained	Mixed baby greens
	Citrus vinaigrette

For the aïoli, combine the egg yolks, lemon juice, garlic, adobo sauce and chipotle chiles in a food processor container. Process until smooth. Add the olive oil gradually, processing constantly until the oil is incorporated and an emulsion is formed. Season with salt and white pepper.

For the crab cakes, sweat the bell peppers, celery and shallot in the olive oil in a skillet. Press the excess moisture from the crab meat. Combine the bell pepper mixture, crab meat, 1 1/2 cups bread crumbs, eggs, egg yolk, parsley, basil, cayenne pepper, salt and pepper in a bowl and mix well. Shape into 8 cylindrical cakes. Coat the cakes with 1 cup bread crumbs. The crab cakes may be stored, covered, in the refrigerator for up to 2 days at this point. Heat an ovenproof sauté pan until smoking. Add the canola oil. Add the crab cakes. Cook until brown; turn. Bake at 350 degrees for 4 minutes.

To serve, toss mixed baby greens with citrus vinaigrette in a bowl. Arrange the greens on each of 8 serving plates. Top each serving with a crab cake. Drizzle with the aïoli.

Yield: 8 servings

Chipotle Shrimp with Cream Sauce

From Doc Martin's Restaurant at The Historic Taos Inn

$1/2$ cup (1 stick) unsalted butter
2 red bell peppers, roasted, peeled, seeded
1 chipotle chile in adobo sauce
2 tablespoons lemon juice
2 tablespoons fish sauce
18 (16 to 20 count) shrimp, peeled, deveined
1 tablespoon olive oil
1 tablespoon minced shallot
1 teaspoon minced garlic
$1/4$ cup white wine
$1/4$ cup heavy cream
Salt and pepper to taste
Griddle Corn Cakes (page 110)

Combine the butter, bell peppers, chipotle chile, lemon juice and fish sauce in a blender container. Process until compound butter is formed. Sauté the shrimp in the olive oil in a large sauté pan over high heat until the shrimp are partially cooked; turn. Stir in the shallot and garlic. Sauté until the shallot and garlic are golden.

Deglaze the sauté pan with the white wine. Cook until the liquid is reduced by $1/2$, stirring constantly. Stir in the heavy cream and simmer, stirring frequently. Add the compound butter and mix well. Simmer until of the desired consistency, stirring frequently. Season with salt and pepper. Drizzle over Griddle Corn Cakes. Serve immediately.

Yield: 4 to 6 servings

The charming and gracious Rancho de San Juan Country Inn & Restaurant was approved for membership in Relais & Châteaux, and is still the only member in the Southwest. Their wine list boasts Wine Spectator's "Award of Excellence."

Marinated Tiger Prawns with Napa Slaw and Red Chile Honey

From Rancho de San Juan

Tiger Prawns

2 cups water	Salt to taste
4 chipotle chiles	16 prawns, shelled, deveined
1 cup olive oil	

Red Chile Honey

1 cup New Mexico honey	2 tablespoons Chimayó
1/4 cup water	ground red chile

Napa Slaw

1/2 cup rice wine vinegar	2 tablespoons black sesame
1/4 cup mirin	seeds
1/4 cup walnut oil	Salt to taste
1 tablespoon sesame oil	1 head napa cabbage,
2 tablespoons water	shredded

For the prawns, combine the water and chipotle chiles in a saucepan. Bring to a simmer. Simmer until the liquid is reduced to 1 cup and the chiles are tender. Drain, reserving the liquid. Remove the stems from the chiles. Process the chiles and reserved liquid in a blender until smooth. Add the olive oil and salt. Process until blended. Pour over the prawns in a shallow dish, turning to coat. Marinate, covered, in the refrigerator for 4 hours, turning occasionally; drain. Grill over hot coals until cooked through.

For the chile honey, combine the honey, water and red chile in a saucepan. Cook until heated through, stirring occasionally.

For the slaw, whisk the wine vinegar, mirin, walnut oil, sesame oil, water, sesame seeds and salt in a bowl. Pour over the cabbage in a bowl and toss to coat.

To serve, arrange 4 prawns, tails facing the center, in a circle on a mound of the slaw on each of 4 serving plates. Drizzle with the chile honey.

Yield: 4 servings

Grilled Shrimp with Citrus Salsa

Citrus Salsa

2 oranges
2 peaches, peeled, chopped
1 jalapeño chile, minced
2 tablespoons minced purple onion
1 tablespoon olive oil
1 tablespoon pickled jalapeño juice
1 garlic clove, minced
1 teaspoon chopped fresh rosemary

Shrimp

1 cup orange juice
1 tablespoon olive oil
1 bunch rosemary, stems removed
5 garlic cloves, chopped
1/4 teaspoon freshly ground pepper
1 to 1 1/2 pounds large or jumbo shrimp, peeled, deveined

For the salsa, grate the zest from the oranges. Peel and separate the oranges into sections and chop. Combine 2 tablespoons of the orange zest, chopped oranges, peaches, jalapeño chile, onion, olive oil, jalapeño juice, garlic and rosemary in a bowl and mix well. Chill, covered, for 3 hours.

For the shrimp, combine the remaining orange zest, orange juice, olive oil, rosemary, garlic and pepper in a shallow dish or sealable plastic bag. Add the shrimp. Cover or seal. Marinate in the refrigerator for 30 minutes, turning occasionally.

Drain the shrimp, reserving the marinade. Thread the shrimp on skewers. Grill the shrimp over medium-high heat for 5 minutes per side, basting with the reserved marinade. Serve with the salsa.

Yield: 4 servings

Mango-Papaya Salsa makes a great accompaniment for the Bourbon-Basted Salmon. Thirty minutes before serving mix 3/4 cup chopped mango, 3/4 cup chopped papaya, 3/4 cup fresh pineapple chunks, 3/4 cup coarsely chopped fresh mint and 1 finely minced seeded jalapeño chile.

Jalapeño Orange Shrimp and Pasta

1/2 cup (1 stick) butter
2 dozen large shrimp, peeled, deveined
2 tablespoons minced green onions
1 fresh or canned jalapeño chile, seeded, chopped
1/2 cup dry white wine

2 cups whipping cream or half-and-half
1 1/2 cups orange juice
Salt and pepper to taste
12 ounces angel hair pasta or spaghetti, cooked
Minced fresh parsley

Heat the butter in a large skillet over medium heat. Add the shrimp. Cook until pink, stirring frequently. Remove the shrimp to a platter with a slotted spoon, reserving the pan drippings. Sauté the green onions and jalapeño chile in the reserved pan drippings for 1 minute. Stir in the wine. Bring to a boil. Stir in the whipping cream and orange juice. Boil for 10 minutes or until the mixture is reduced to the consistency of a thin sauce, stirring occasionally. Season with salt and pepper. Stir in the shrimp. Cook just until heated through, stirring frequently. Pour over the hot cooked pasta in a bowl and toss to mix. Sprinkle with parsley.

Yield: 4 servings

Bourbon-Basted Salmon

4 (6-ounce) salmon fillets, bones removed
1/4 cup packed brown sugar
1/4 cup bourbon

1/4 cup soy sauce
1/4 cup vegetable oil
1/4 cup chopped green onions

Arrange the salmon in a single layer in a shallow dish. Combine the brown sugar, bourbon, soy sauce, oil and green onions in a bowl and mix well. Pour over the salmon, turning to coat. Marinate, covered, in the refrigerator for 1 hour, turning occasionally. Drain the salmon, reserving the marinade. Place the salmon in a grilling basket. Grill over hot coals for 7 minutes per side or until the salmon flakes easily, turning once and basting with the reserved marinade several times. Serve hot or cold with Mango-Papaya Salsa.

Yield: 4 servings

Grilled Salmon with Avocado Salsa

From The Artichoke Café

Avocado Salsa

1 firm ripe avocado, chopped
2 large firm tomatoes, seeded, finely chopped
1/2 small red onion, finely chopped
Juice of 1/2 lime
2 tablespoons chopped fresh cilantro leaves
1/8 teaspoon Tabasco sauce
Salt and freshly ground pepper to taste

Salmon

6 salmon fillets
3 tablespoons olive oil
1 tablespoon lemon juice
Salt and pepper to taste
Chopped fresh parsley to taste
Chopped garlic to taste

For the salsa, combine the avocado, tomatoes, onion, lime juice, cilantro, Tabasco sauce, salt and pepper in a bowl and mix gently.

For the salmon, arrange the salmon in a single layer in a shallow dish. Whisk the olive oil, lemon juice, salt, pepper, parsley and garlic in a bowl. Pour over the salmon, turning to coat. Marinate in the refrigerator for 10 to 15 minutes.

Preheat the grill on high. Brush the rack with oil. Reduce the heat to medium. Arrange the salmon diagonally on the rack and close the lid. Grill for 3 to 5 minutes. Turn the fillets to face the opposite direction to ensure nice grill marks. Grill for 3 minutes longer; turn. Grill for 5 minutes per inch of thickness, or less for rare. Serve with the salsa.

Yield: 6 servings

Blue Corn Trout with Ancho Chile Pesto

From Doc Martin's Restaurant at The Historic Taos Inn

Ancho Chile Pesto

4 ancho chiles, hydrated, seeded, stemmed
1 cup sun-dried tomatoes, hydrated
2 roasted red bell peppers, peeled, seeded
1/2 cup sliced almonds, toasted

1/2 cup pine nuts, toasted
1/2 cup loosely packed fresh basil
2 tablespoons sesame seeds, toasted
2 tablespoons olive oil
1 tablespoon molasses
1 tablespoon lemon juice

Trout and Assembly

6 trout fillets
Salt and pepper to taste
BUENO® blue corn flour

Vegetable oil for frying
Fish stock or water

For the pesto, combine the ancho chiles, sun-dried tomatoes, roasted bell peppers, almonds, pine nuts, basil, sesame seeds, olive oil, molasses and lemon juice in a food processor fitted with a metal blade. Process until smooth.

For the trout, sprinkle both sides of the fillets with salt and pepper. Coat with the blue corn flour. Panfry the trout in a small amount of oil in a sauté pan for 2 minutes per side or until the trout flakes easily; drain. Remove to a platter. Cover to keep warm.

To assemble, pan roast the pesto in a sauté pan over medium-high heat, stirring frequently. Add just enough fish stock or water until of the consistency of a thin sauce. Season with salt and pepper. Cook just until heated through, stirring constantly. Drizzle over the trout. Serve immediately.

Yield: 6 servings

Southwestern Blackened Ahi Tuna with Warm Wasabi

From Martin Rios of The Old House

Southwest Spice

3 tablespoons BUENO® red chile powder
2 tablespoons brown sugar
1 tablespoon curry powder
1 tablespoon cayenne pepper
1 teaspoon dried thyme
1 teaspoon dried basil
1/2 teaspoon cinnamon
1/2 teaspoon dry mustard

Warm Wasabi Sushi Salad

1 pound short grain sushi rice
2 cups water
1/4 cup rice vinegar
2 tablespoons sugar
1 small yellow tomato, coarsely chopped
1 small red tomato, coarsely chopped
10 asparagus tips, coarsely chopped
2 tablespoons walnut oil
1 tablespoon wasabi powder
1 tablespoon rice vinegar

Red Curry Carrot Sauce

1 tablespoon olive oil
1 small onion, chopped
2 medium carrots, chopped
1 rib celery, chopped
1 garlic clove
3 cups clam juice
1 tablespoon red curry paste
1/4 cup (1/2 stick) butter, chilled
Salt and pepper to taste

Ahi Tuna and Assembly
4 (4- to 5-ounce) Ahi tuna fillets
Bean Sprouts
Chives

For the spice, combine the red chile powder, brown sugar, curry powder, cayenne pepper, thyme, basil, cinnamon and dry mustard in a jar with a tight-fitting lid. Shake to mix.

For the salad, rinse the rice in a colander under running water until the water runs clear. Place the rice in an electric rice cooker. Stir in 2 cups water, 1/4 cup rice vinegar and sugar. Cook until the rice is tender and sticky. Remove the rice to a bowl. Stir in the tomatoes, asparagus, walnut oil, wasabi powder and 1 tablespoon rice vinegar. Cover to keep warm.

For the sauce, heat the olive oil in a medium saucepan until hot. Stir in the onion, carrots, celery and garlic. Cook until the vegetables are tender, stirring occasionally. Add the clam juice and red curry paste and mix well. Cook until the liquid is reduced to 2 cups, stirring frequently. Process the vegetable mixture in a blender until puréed. Add the butter. Process until blended. Season with salt and pepper. Return the sauce to the saucepan. Cover to keep warm.

For the tuna, coat the surface of the fillets with the spice mixture. Heat a sauté pan over high heat. Add the fillets. Sear until blackened on both sides.

To assemble, spoon a mound of the salad in the center of each of 4 serving plates. Slice the tuna and arrange next to the salad. Drizzle with 1 cup of the sauce. Top with bean sprouts and chives.

Yield: 4 servings

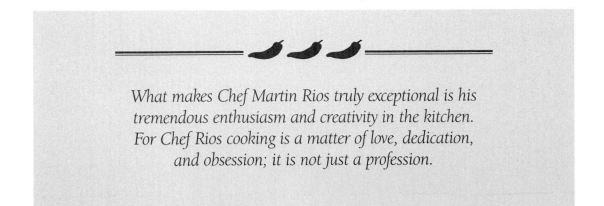

What makes Chef Martin Rios truly exceptional is his tremendous enthusiasm and creativity in the kitchen. For Chef Rios cooking is a matter of love, dedication, and obsession; it is not just a profession.

Pumpkin Ravioli

From The Artichoke Café

Filling

1 pound finely chopped peeled butternut squash
1 (2 1/2-pound) package fresh spinach, blanched, finely chopped
10 cups ricotta cheese
1 cup freshly grated Parmesan cheese
1/8 teaspoon freshly grated nutmeg
Salt and white pepper to taste

Ravioli

2 cups all-purpose flour
1 cup semolina flour
4 extra-large eggs
1/3 cup puréed cooked pumpkin
1/4 cup olive oil
2 eggs, beaten
2 to 4 tablespoons water

Roasted Tomato Sauce and Assembly

1/2 cup (1 stick) butter
1 cup chopped roasted Roma tomatoes
1/2 cup chopped hazelnuts, toasted
1 tablespoon chopped fresh sage
Salt and pepper to taste
Freshly grated Parmesan cheese to taste

For the filling, steam the squash until tender-crisp; drain. Mix the squash, spinach, ricotta cheese, Parmesan cheese, nutmeg, salt and white pepper in a bowl.

For the pasta, combine the all-purpose flour, semolina flour, 4 extra-large eggs, pumpkin and olive oil in a food processor container. Process for 45 seconds or until the mixture forms a ball. If the dough comes together in a sticky mass in just a few seconds, it is too moist. Separate the dough into several pieces and sprinkle with a few tablespoons additional flour. Process for 30 seconds longer. If the dough forms large crumbs and does not adhere in a ball, press some of the crumbs together. If they stick, then the dough is of the right consistency. If the crumbs are small and dry, add a few teaspoons of beaten egg or water and process for 30 seconds longer. Knead on a lightly floured surface for 5 seconds. If rolling the dough by hand, dust with flour and wrap in plastic wrap. Let rest for 30 minutes so the gluten will relax and the dough will be easier to roll.

To roll using a pasta machine, separate the dough into 2 equal portions. Wrap 1 portion and place in the refrigerator until needed. Set the rollers of the pasta machine on the widest notch. Flatten a piece of the remaining dough with your hands and pass it through the rollers of the pasta machine. Fold the dough into thirds, press it together and dust lightly with flour. Feed 1 of the open ends of the dough through the machine. Repeat this process several times. Move the setting of the pasta machine to the next notch. This time do not fold the dough. Dust with flour on 1 side and roll it through the machine. Continue to flatten the pasta, moving the rollers 1 notch closer each time. When the rollers are on the thinnest setting, dust the dough with flour on both sides and pass it through the machine. Repeat the process with the remaining dough.

Arrange 1 strip of the dough on the ravioli mold. Brush with a mixture of 2 eggs and the water. Fill each section with some of the filling. Top with another strip of pasta. Roll with a small wooden rolling pin. Turn onto a lightly floured cutting board and separate the ravioli sections. Place the finished ravioli on a baking sheet dusted with flour. Repeat the process with the remaining pasta, filling and egg wash. You may store the ravioli in the refrigerator for several hours or freeze for future use at this point.

For the sauce, heat the butter in a large sauté pan over medium heat until almost brown. Stir in the tomatoes, hazelnuts, sage, salt and pepper. Cook until heated through and of the desired consistency, stirring frequently. Remove from heat. Cover to keep warm.

To assemble, cook the ravioli in boiling salted water in a stockpot for 7 minutes or just until tender; drain. Arrange the ravioli in individual pasta bowls. Drizzle with the sauce and sprinkle with Parmesan cheese.

Yield: 6 servings

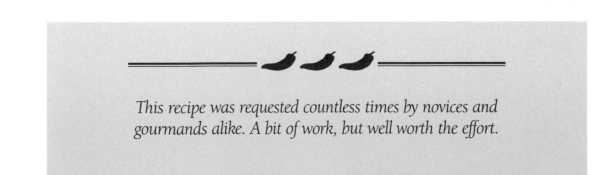

This recipe was requested countless times by novices and gourmands alike. A bit of work, but well worth the effort.

Sweet Corn and Mushroom Tamales

From Coyote Café

Sweet Corn Masa

2 ears of corn	1/2 teaspoon salt
2 tablespoons unsalted	1/2 teaspoon freshly ground
butter, softened	pepper
2/3 to 1 cup cornmeal	1/4 cup grated Parmesan cheese
1 egg	2 tablespoons chopped
1 teaspoon sugar	jalapeño chiles

Mushroom Pepper Filling

2 large portobellos (8 ounces)	2 red bell peppers, roasted,
1 1/2 tablespoons olive oil	peeled, seeded, chopped
3/4 cup thinly sliced	2 green bell peppers, roasted,
chanterelles (3 ounces)	peeled, seeded, chopped
2 tablespoons chopped fresh	2 cups shredded smoked
marjoram	Gouda cheese
2 yellow bell peppers,	1/2 teaspoon salt
roasted, peeled, seeded,	1/2 teaspoon freshly ground
chopped	pepper

Tamales

12 to 16 BUENO® dried	2 cups Salsa Supreme
corn husks	(page 195)

For the masa, cut the corn kernels from the ears of corn and scrape the ears with the back of a knife to squeeze out as much of the corn germ and corn milk as possible. Combine the corn kernels, scraped germ and butter in a food processor container. Process until smooth. Add 2/3 cup of the cornmeal, egg, sugar, salt, pepper and Parmesan cheese. Pulse until blended, scraping the side of the bowl as needed. Add the remaining 1/3 cup cornmeal as needed to soak up the excess liquid so the masa will adhere. Taste and adjust the seasonings. Fold in the jalapeño chiles. Let stand, wrapped in plastic wrap, at room temperature for 30 minutes.

For the filling, brush the portobellos with some of the olive oil. Arrange in a single layer on a baking sheet. Roast at 350 degrees for 5 to 6 minutes or until tender.

Chop the portobellos into 1/4-inch pieces. Sauté the chanterelles in the remaining olive oil in a skillet over medium heat for 2 to 3 minutes. Add 1 tablespoon water if needed to prevent scorching. Drain the mushrooms. Let stand until cool. Toss the mushrooms, marjoram, bell peppers and cheese in a bowl. Season with the salt and pepper. Chill, covered, in the refrigerator.

For the tamales, soak the corn husks in enough warm water to cover in a bowl for 20 minutes. Drain and shake to remove the excess moisture. Spread the corn husks on a clean, hard surface. If the corn husks are small, lay 1 over the other, slightly overlapping. Divide the masa evenly among the husks. Spread the masa out in a rectangular shape, leaving room to gather and tie the husk at the tapered end. Divide the mushroom filling evenly among the tamales and place over the masa, making a line of it down the center. Roll the tamale into the tightest possible cylinder, being careful not to roll the husk into the center of the tamale. Tear a strip of husk and use it to tie the tapered end snugly. The tamales can be prepared up to 24 hours in advance and stored, covered, in the refrigerator.

Steam the tamales for 30 to 35 minutes over simmering water. It is very important that little or no steam escape while cooking and that the tamales not be crowded. The tamales are done when they feel firm to the touch but are not hard and the dough comes away easily from the husk. Let stand for 5 minutes. Serve with the salsa.

Yield: 12 tamales

Mark Miller and the Coyote Café treat patrons to the latest in Southwestern-infused cuisine.

Five-Chile Dippin' Sauce

From Jim White's "Kitchen Minute"

1/2 cup soy sauce
1/2 cup vinegar
2 tablespoons raspberry
preserves
1 tablespoon Worcestershire
sauce
1 tablespoon Tabasco sauce
1 teaspoon salt

1/2 teaspoon minced
habanero chile
1/2 teaspoon minced
chipotle chile
1/2 teaspoon black pepper
1/2 teaspoon red chile
1/2 teaspoon powdered
green chile

Combine the soy sauce, vinegar, raspberry preserves, Worcestershire sauce, Tabasco sauce, salt, habanero chile, chipotle chile, black pepper, red chile and green chile in a bowl and mix well.

Yield: 1 1/2 cups

Papaya and Balsamic Marinade

From Jim White's "Kitchen Minute"

1 large ripe papaya, peeled,
chopped
1 cup Italian salad dressing
1/2 cup balsamic vinegar
1/4 cup tequila
1 tablespoon seasoned salt

1 tablespoon mango chutney
1 tablespoon salt
1 tablespoon Tabasco sauce
2 garlic cloves
1 large sprig of thyme, stem
removed

Combine the papaya, salad dressing, balsamic vinegar, tequila, seasoned salt, chutney, salt, Tabasco sauce, garlic and thyme in a food processor container. Process until smooth.

Yield: 2 cups

Oriental Marinade

155

From Jim White's "Kitchen Minute"

1 cup soy sauce
Juice of 1 orange
1/4 cup chile oil
1/4 cup minced gingerroot
2 tablespoons black soy sauce
2 tablespoons A.1. steak sauce

2 tablespoons black bean & garlic sauce
2 tablespoons peanut butter
1 tablespoon hot chile sauce
1 tablespoon Worcestershire sauce
1 tablespoon sesame oil
4 garlic cloves, minced

Whisk the soy sauce, orange juice, chile oil, gingerroot, black soy sauce, A.1. steak sauce, black bean & garlic sauce, peanut butter, hot chile sauce, Worcestershire sauce, sesame oil and garlic in a bowl. Let stand for 2 hours before using.

Yield: 3 cups

Vegetable Marinade

From Jim White's "Kitchen Minute"

1/4 cup olive oil
2 tablespoons apple syrup
2 tablespoons dry salsa mix
2 tablespoons chipotle paste

Juice of 2 limes
1/8 teaspoon granulated garlic
1/8 teaspoon seasoned salt

Combine the olive oil, syrup, salsa mix, chipotle paste, lime juice, granulated garlic and seasoned salt in a bowl and mix well. Marinate your favorite vegetables for 1 hour or longer before grilling. The flavor is enhanced if the vegetables are allowed to marinate for 8 to 10 hours.

Yield: 3/4 cup

Enchanted Endings

Desserts

Art and Soul

T hanks to its historical past and artistic present, Canyon Road is known as the "Art and Soul of Santa Fe." Its reputation as an artist colony stems from the legacy of five young artists who in 1920 vowed to bring art to the people of Sante Fe. They named themselves Los Cincos Pintores and painted their way into American art history with their robust and romantic canvases.

Strolling Canyon Road is a Christmas Eve tradition that is dear to our hearts. Gallery windows are lighted as a sign of welcome to passers-by. Hundreds of candles placed in small paper bags filled with sand, fondly called farolitos, illuminate the walk up Canyon Road. Spontaneous bonfires are built along the way, the pungent smell of piñon smoke encompasses the area, and carolers gather to bring yuletide joy and well wishes.

After our pilgrimage up the road, we return to our own hearths, fill ourselves with splendid desserts, and prepare to usher in Christmas Day.

Sweetness Defined

Dessert Buffet for Friends & Family

Chocolate Hazelnut Heaven

Banana Cheesecake with Hazelnut Crust

Fudgy Raspberry Bars

Sublime Blueberry Tart

Turtle Sundae Torte

Serve with flavored coffee and assorted liqueurs.

The Heart of the Matter

Easy Dinner for Dessert Lovers

Cream of Avocado Soup

Festive Romaine Salad

Banana Enchiladas

Black Mesa Pie

Toasted Coconut Bread

Add fresh berries and whipped cream to finish out this

quick and easy dinner.

Banana Enchiladas

From Double Eagle Restaurant

2 cups whipping cream
2 tablespoons sugar
1 teaspoon vanilla extract
6 bananas, cut horizontally into halves
1 package commercially prepared crepes
2 (12-ounce) jars caramel ice cream sauce
1 quart vanilla ice cream

Beat the whipping cream in a chilled mixing bowl with chilled beaters until soft peaks form. Add the sugar and vanilla and mix well. Chill, covered, in the refrigerator.

Roll each banana half in a crepe. Spoon some of the caramel sauce in the center of each of 6 dessert plates. Arrange 2 crepe-wrapped bananas over the sauce on each plate. Top with a scoop of ice cream and drizzle with caramel sauce. Top with the whipped cream. Serve immediately.

Commercially prepared crepes are found in the frozen pastry sections of most grocery stores.

Yield: 6 servings

Chocolate Liquid-Center Cake

From Martin Rios of The Old House

8 ounces bittersweet chocolate
1 cup (2 sticks) butter
9 eggs
7 ounces egg yolks
8 ounces sugar
6 ounces flour

Combine the chocolate and butter in a double boiler over simmering water. Simmer until blended, stirring occasionally.

Beat the eggs and egg yolks in a mixing bowl until light and fluffy. Add the sugar 4 ounces at a time, beating well after each addition. Add the chocolate mixture and mix well. Add the flour gradually, beating constantly until blended.

Brush four 4- or 5-ounce ramekins with melted butter. Fill the ramekins 3/4 full with the batter. Bake at 370 degrees for 6 to 7 minutes. Invert each ramekin onto a dessert plate. Serve with vanilla sauce or vanilla ice cream.

Yield: 4 servings

*One of the most often requested desserts at The Old House,
this cake's soft, buttery center oozes onto the plate, inducing
sheer giddiness in its diners.*

Pumpkin Cheesecake

$1/2$ cup gingersnap cookie crumbs
$1/2$ cup walnut or pecan pieces
16 ounces reduced-fat cream cheese, softened
$1^1/2$ cups sugar
6 eggs
$1/3$ cup flour
$1^1/2$ teaspoons cinnamon
1 teaspoon nutmeg
1 teaspoon ground cloves
$1/4$ teaspoon allspice
$1/8$ teaspoon salt
2 cups packed pumpkin purée
Whipped cream (optional)

Combine the cookie crumbs and walnuts in a bowl and mix well. Sprinkle over the bottom of a buttered 9-inch springform pan. Chill in the refrigerator.

Beat the cream cheese, sugar, eggs, flour, cinnamon, nutmeg, cloves, allspice and salt in a mixing bowl until smooth. Add the pumpkin purée and beat until blended. Spoon into the prepared pan.

Bake at 325 degrees for $1^1/2$ hours. Turn off the oven. Let the cheesecake stand in oven with door open for 30 minutes. Remove to a wire rack to cool completely. Store, covered, in the refrigerator until serving time. Top each serving with a dollop of whipped cream.

Yield: 10 to 12 servings

Banana Cheesecake with Hazelnut Crust

From Terra American Bistro

Hazelnut Crust

1 1/2 cups hazelnuts, toasted, ground
1 1/2 cups plain bread crumbs
1/4 cup (1/2 stick) butter, melted

Banana Filling

12 ounces mascarpone cheese
1 cup sour cream
4 ounces cream cheese, softened
1 tablespoon vanilla extract
3/4 cup sugar
1/2 cup puréed bananas
4 eggs
1/4 cup plus 2 tablespoons sifted cornstarch
1/8 teaspoon salt
Crème fraîche (optional)
Fresh berries (optional)

For the crust, preheat the oven to 350 degrees.. Combine the hazelnuts, bread crumbs and butter in a bowl and mix well. Pat the crumb mixture over the bottom and up the side of a greased 10-inch springform pan. Bake for 10 minutes.

For the filling, beat the mascarpone cheese, sour cream, cream cheese and vanilla in a mixing bowl just until blended. Add the sugar, bananas and eggs 1 at a time, beating constantly until smooth. Add the cornstarch and salt and mix well. Spoon into the prepared pan.

Reduce the oven temperature to 325 degrees. Bake for 1 hour. Cool in pan on a wire rack. Store, covered, in the refrigerator. Top with crème fraîche and fresh berries just before serving.

Yield: 12 servings

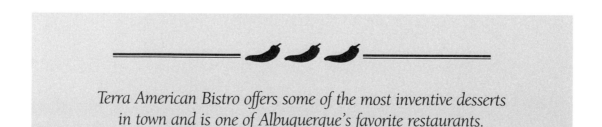

Terra American Bistro offers some of the most inventive desserts in town and is one of Albuquerque's favorite restaurants.

Bread Pudding
Capirotada

8 slices bread, toasted
2 cups water
1 cup sugar
1 teaspoon cinnamon
$1/2$ teaspoon nutmeg
$1/2$ teaspoon ground cloves
$1/4$ teaspoon salt
$1^1/2$ cups shredded Cheddar cheese
$1^1/2$ cups raisins
2 tablespoons butter, cut into pieces
Whipped cream (optional)

Break the toasted bread into 2-inch pieces. Combine the water, sugar, cinnamon, nutmeg, cloves and salt in a saucepan. Bring to a boil; reduce heat. Simmer for 10 minutes, stirring occasionally.

Layer the bread, cheese, raisins and butter in a buttered shallow baking pan. Pour the syrup mixture over the top. Bake at 350 degrees for 20 minutes or until the syrup is absorbed. Serve warm or cold topped with whipped cream.

Yield: 6 to 8 servings

Green Chile Apple Cobbler

From Jim White's "Kitchen Minute"

Apple Filling

5 or 6 apples, chopped	1/4 teaspoon cinnamon
2/3 cup packed brown sugar	1/8 teaspoon salt
1/2 cup green chile	1/8 teaspoon allspice
1 teaspoon cider vinegar	1/8 teaspoon nutmeg

Topping

1 cup sugar	1/8 teaspoon cinnamon
1 cup flour	1/8 teaspoon nutmeg
Grated zest of 1 lemon	1 cup (2 sticks) butter, cubed
1/8 teaspoon salt	2 tablespoons heavy cream

For the filling, combine the apples, brown sugar, green chile, vinegar, cinnamon, salt, allspice and nutmeg in a bowl and mix well. Spoon into a greased baking pan.

For the topping, combine the sugar, flour, lemon zest, salt, cinnamon and nutmeg in a bowl and mix well. Cut in the butter until crumbly. Stir in the heavy cream. Spread the topping over the prepared layer and press firmly to pack. Bake at 375 degrees until brown and bubbly.

Yield: 6 to 8 servings

*We know this recipe for Green Chile Apple Cobbler seems like
a strange combination of flavors, but it is truly a delight.*

Bailey's Chocolate Chip Ice Cream

3 egg yolks
3/4 cup sugar
1/2 cup whipping cream
1 teaspoon vanilla extract
1/4 cup Bailey's Irish cream
4 ounces semisweet chocolate, melted
2 cups whipping cream
3 egg whites

Combine the egg yolks, sugar, 1/2 cup whipping cream and vanilla in a double boiler over simmering water. Whisk for 8 to 10 minutes or until the mixture is hot and the sugar has dissolved.

Fill a medium bowl halfway with ice and water. Set on a wet tea towel. Pour the hot egg yolk mixture into a small bowl and place the bowl in the ice bath. Spin the bowl, stirring constantly with a rubber spatula for 10 minutes or until the yolk mixture thickens and becomes very cold. Stir in the Irish cream. Add the warm chocolate, mixing constantly with a rubber spatula until blended; the chocolate will clump. Keep the mixture in the ice bath.

Beat 2 cups whipping cream in mixing bowl at medium speed until soft peaks form. Chill, covered, in the refrigerator. Beat the egg whites in a mixing bowl until stiff peaks form. Fold the beaten egg whites into the chilled whipped cream. Fold in the chocolate mixture.

Spoon the chocolate mixture into a 2- or 3-quart aluminum bowl or shallow glass dish. Freeze, covered, for 8 hours or until firm. Let stand at room temperature for 5 to 10 minutes before serving.

Yield: 8 to 10 servings

Five-Minute Peach Sherbet

1 (20-ounce) package frozen sliced peaches
1 cup yogurt
1 cup confectioners' sugar
1 tablespoon fresh lemon juice
1/4 teaspoon almond extract

Place the peaches in a food processor container fitted with a steel blade. Process until of the consistency of shaved ice. Add the yogurt, confectioners' sugar, lemon juice and flavoring. Process until of the consistency of sherbet, scraping the bowl occasionally. Serve immediately or freeze for future use. Let frozen sherbet stand at room temperature for 30 minutes before serving.

Yield: 4 cups

*The proud heritage of North America's first inhabitants was
firmly set inside New Mexico with the Anasazi cliff dwellers, who
mysteriously and completely disappeared around 1300 A.D.
Today, more than twenty distinct pueblos and tribes inhabit New Mexico.
All maintain separate and sovereign governments.*

Poached Pears with White Chocolate

1 bottle riesling
2 cups sugar
2 bay leaves
1 vanilla bean
6 Bartlett pears with stems
1 cup whipping cream
10 ounces white chocolate, finely chopped

Bring the wine, sugar, bay leaves and vanilla bean to a simmer in a large saucepan over medium heat. Peel the pears, leaving the stems intact. Remove the cores from the bottom of the pears.

Poach the pears in the simmering wine mixture for 20 minutes or until tender. Remove the pears with a slotted spoon to a platter. Let stand until cool.

Bring the whipping cream to a boil in a saucepan over medium-high heat. Remove from heat. Add the white chocolate gradually, whisking constantly until blended.

Cut a small slice from the bottom of each pear so the pears will stand upright. Place the pears upright in a shallow dish. Ladle the ganache over each pear until coated. Garnish with sprigs of fresh mint and/or fresh raspberries.

Yield: 6 servings

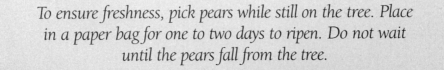

To ensure freshness, pick pears while still on the tree. Place in a paper bag for one to two days to ripen. Do not wait until the pears fall from the tree.

Raspberry Mousse

From Los Poblanos Inn

^{2}/3 cup frozen raspberries, thawed
^{1}/2 cup whipping cream
1 tablespoon sugar
Assorted melons
Kiwifruit
Strawberries
Chopped fresh mint

Process the raspberries in a blender or food processor until puréed. Strain if desired through a fine sieve. Beat the whipping cream in a mixing bowl until soft peaks form. Add the sugar and mix well. Fold into the raspberry purée. Spoon into a bowl.

Scoop out the melons with a melon baller. Peel the kiwifruit and cut each into 2 or 3 pieces. Thread the melon, kiwifruit and strawberries alternately on bamboo skewers and arrange the skewers in a circle on a large platter. Place the mousse in the middle of the platter for dipping. Sprinkle fresh mint over the fruit.

Yield: Variable

*When the raspberries are ripe and come to the Los Ranchos
de Albuquerque Growers Market, I buy as many flats as I
can fit in the back of the van. We eat one flat immediately, make
jams and jellies with some, and freeze the remaining. I use
the fruit to make a raspberry mousse to accompany fruit skewers.
This fabulous dessert may be prepared one day in advance.*

Turtle Sundae Torte

2^1/$_2$ cups graham cracker crumbs
^{1}/$_2$ cup sugar
^{1}/$_2$ cup (1 stick) butter, softened
8 ounces cream cheese, softened
8 ounces whipped topping
^{2}/$_3$ cup confectioners' sugar
Hot fudge ice cream sauce
Caramel ice cream sauce
Chopped pecans

Combine the graham cracker crumbs, sugar and butter in a bowl and mix well. Press the crumb mixture over the bottom of a 9×13-inch baking pan. Bake at 350 degrees for 10 minutes. Let stand until cool.

Beat the cream cheese, whipped topping and confectioners' sugar in a mixing bowl until smooth. Spread the cream cheese mixture over the baked layer. Drizzle with hot fudge ice cream sauce and caramel ice cream sauce. Sprinkle with pecans. Store, covered, in the refrigerator until serving time.

Yield: 12 to 15 servings

Velarde Apple Cake

1 cup sugar
1 cup flour
1 teaspoon baking soda
$1/2$ teaspoon cinnamon
$1/4$ teaspoon nutmeg
$1/2$ cup chopped walnuts
$1/4$ cup ($1/2$ stick) butter, melted
2 eggs, lightly beaten
$1^{1}/3$ cups apple slices

Combine the sugar, flour, baking soda, cinnamon and nutmeg in a bowl and mix well. Stir in the walnuts, butter and eggs. Fold in the apples.

Spoon the batter into a greased 9- or 10-inch round baking dish. Bake at 350 degrees for 40 minutes.

Yield: 6 to 8 servings

Apples have been cultivated in New Mexico since their introduction in 1620 by Spanish priests who planted them to experience a taste of their native Europe.

Chocolate Hazelnut Heaven

From Mia Maes-Blankenau of Until We Eat Again

Simple Syrup

1 cup water   1 tablespoon vanilla extract
1 cup sugar

Cake

1 cup hazelnuts   1½ cups (3 sticks) unsalted
1½ cups dark chocolate   butter, softened
3 cups flour   1¾ cups sugar
1 tablespoon baking   1½ tablespoons vanilla
powder   extract
1 teaspoon baking soda   4 eggs
½ teaspoon salt   1½ cups sour cream

For the syrup, bring the water and sugar to a boil in a saucepan. Boil until the sugar dissolves, stirring occasionally. Remove from heat. Stir in the vanilla. Let stand until cool.

For the cake, spray a bundt pan with nonstick cooking spray or coat with butter and dust with flour. Spread the hazelnuts on a baking sheet. Roast at 450 degrees for 7 minutes or just until they begin to brown; do not burn. Wrap the hazelnuts in a clean tea towel to allow to steam. Reduce the oven temperature to 350 degrees.

Unwrap the tea towel slightly and vigorously rub the towel with the hazelnuts between your hands until the skins come free from the nuts. Repeat if necessary. Coarsely chop the hazelnuts.

Pulse the chocolate in a food processor until finely chopped. Combine the flour, baking powder, baking soda and salt in a bowl and mix well. Beat the butter and sugar in a mixing bowl until creamy. Beat in the vanilla. Add the eggs 1 at a time, beating well after each addition. Add the dry ingredients and mix well. Stir in the chocolate and hazelnuts. Fold in the sour cream.

Spoon the batter into the prepared pan. Bake at 350 degrees for 50 to 60 minutes or until a wooden pick inserted in the center comes out clean. Cool in pan on a wire rack for 20 minutes. Invert onto a serving plate. Brush the entire surface of the cake with the syrup. Let stand until cool. Chill, covered in plastic wrap, for 8 to 10 hours before serving to allow the flavors to meld.

Yield: 16 servings

Coconut Sour Cream Cake

1 (2-layer) package butter-flavor cake mix
2 cups sour cream
2 cups sugar
12 ounces shredded coconut
1¹/2 cups frozen whipped topping, thawed
Strawberries

Prepare and bake the cake using package directions for two 9-inch round cake pans. Cool in pans for 10 minutes. Remove to a wire rack to cool completely. Cut each cake layer horizontally into halves.

Combine the sour cream, sugar and coconut in a bowl and mix well. Chill, covered, in the refrigerator. Reserve 1 cup of the sour cream mixture. Spread the remaining sour cream mixture between the cake layers.

Combine the reserved sour cream mixture and whipped topping in a bowl and mix well. Spread over the top and side of the cake. Place the cake in an airtight container. Chill for 3 days before serving. Garnish with fresh strawberries.

Yield: 12 servings

Adobe Pound Cake

1 cup (2 sticks) butter, softened
1 cup plus 2 tablespoons sugar
6 egg yolks, beaten
2 cups flour
$1/2$ teaspoon Mexican vanilla extract
$1/2$ teaspoon almond extract
$1/8$ teaspoon mace
6 egg whites

Beat the butter in a mixing bowl until creamy. Add half the sugar. Beat until creamy. Add the remaining sugar and beat until light and fluffy. Add half the egg yolks. Beat until blended. Add half the flour. Beat until creamy. Add the remaining egg yolks. Beat until creamy. Beat in the remaining flour until blended. Add the flavorings and mace and beat until blended.

Beat the egg whites in a mixing bowl until soft peaks form. Fold into the batter. Spoon the batter into a greased and floured bundt pan. Place the pan in a cold oven. Bake at 250 degrees for $2^{1/2}$ hours. Cool in pan for 10 minutes. Remove to a wire rack to cool completely. Spread with butter icing and decorate as desired.

Yield: 15 to 20 servings

To make a delicious homemade version of vanilla extract follow these simple instructions. Combine a split vanilla bean and $3/4$ cup vodka in a jar with a tight-fitting lid. Seal tightly and store in a cool dark environment for four to six months, shaking occasionally.

Black Mesa Pie

3/4 cup sugar
1/2 cup (1 stick) butter, softened
1 ounce unsweetened chocolate, melted, cooled
1 teaspoon Mexican vanilla extract
2 eggs
1 baked (8-inch) pie shell
Whipped cream

Beat the sugar and butter in a mixing bowl until creamy. Add the chocolate and vanilla and mix well. Add the eggs 1 at a time, beating 5 minutes after each addition. Spoon the chocolate mixture into the pie shell. Chill, covered, in the refrigerator until set. Top with whipped cream.

For a 10-inch pie, combine 1 cup plus 2 tablespoons sugar, 3/4 cup butter, 1 1/2 ounces chocolate, 1 1/2 teaspoons Mexican vanilla extract and 3 eggs. Spoon into a 10-inch baked pie shell.

To avoid raw eggs that may carry salmonella, we suggest using an equivalent amount of pasteurized egg substitute.

Yield: 6 to 8 servings

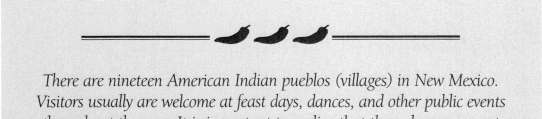

There are nineteen American Indian pueblos (villages) in New Mexico. Visitors usually are welcome at feast days, dances, and other public events throughout the year. It is important to realize that these dances are not only social, but are religious events to be observed with respect.

French Apple Pie

From The Pink Adobe

Crust

2 cups flour

1 teaspoon salt

3/4 cup lard

6 to 7 tablespoons cold water

Apple Filling

1 pound fresh apples, peeled, sliced, or 1 (16-ounce) can sliced apples, drained

2 tablespoons fresh lemon juice

1/2 teaspoon nutmeg

1/2 teaspoon cinnamon

1/2 cup sugar

1/4 cup raisins

1 cup packed brown sugar

2 tablespoons flour

2 tablespoons butter, softened

1/2 cup pecan pieces

1/4 cup milk

Hard Sauce

1/2 cup (1 stick) butter

1 1/2 cups confectioners' sugar

1 tablespoon boiling water

1 teaspoon brandy or rum

For the crust, combine the flour and salt in a bowl and mix well. Cut in the lard until crumbly. Add the cold water gradually, mixing until the dough adheres. Divide the dough into 2 equal portions. Roll 1 portion into a 12-inch circle on a lightly floured surface. Fit into a 9-inch pie plate. Roll the remaining portion for the top crust and set aside.

For the filling, arrange the apples in the pastry-lined pie plate and drizzle with the lemon juice. Sprinkle with the nutmeg and cinnamon. Spread the sugar evenly over the apples and sprinkle with the raisins. Combine the brown sugar, flour and butter in a bowl and mix well. Spread over the prepared layers. Sprinkle with the pecans. Drizzle with 3 tablespoons of the milk. Top with the remaining pastry, sealing the edge. Prick the top of the pastry with a fork and brush with the remaining 1 tablespoon milk. Bake at 450 degrees for 10 minutes then reduce heat to 350 degrees and bake for 30 minutes or until golden brown.

For the sauce, beat the butter in a mixing bowl until light and fluffy. Add the confectioners' sugar and boiling water and beat until blended. Beat in the brandy until smooth. Top each serving with some of the sauce.

Yield: 6 servings

Gingersnap Pie

Crust
1 cup gingersnap crumbs
2 tablespoons butter, softened

Filling
1 quart vanilla ice cream, slightly softened
1 (2-ounce) Heath candy bar, crushed

Sauce and Assembly
$1/2$ cup packed brown sugar
$1/2$ cup whipping cream
$1/4$ cup ($1/2$ stick) butter or margarine
1 teaspoon vanilla extract
$1/4$ cup chopped almonds, toasted

For the crust, combine the gingersnap crumbs and butter in a bowl and mix well. Pat the crumb mixture over the bottom and up the side of a pie plate. Freeze for 10 minutes.

For the filling, combine the ice cream and candy bar in a bowl and mix well. Spoon into the prepared pie plate. Freeze, covered, for 8 to 10 hours.

For the sauce, combine the brown sugar, whipping cream, butter and vanilla in a saucepan. Bring just to a boil, stirring frequently.

To assemble, cut the pie into 6 to 8 wedges. Arrange each wedge on a dessert plate. Drizzle with the sauce and sprinkle with the almonds. Serve immediately.

Yield: 6 to 8 servings

Sublime Blueberry Tart

Crust

1¹/₂ cups unbleached flour
¹/₄ cup sugar
¹/₈ teaspoon salt
7 tablespoons shortening, chilled

5 tablespoons unsalted butter, chilled
6 tablespoons (about) cold water

Filling

1¹/₂ cups blanched slivered almonds
1 cup sugar
1 egg

¹/₂ cup (1 stick) unsalted butter, softened
1¹/₂ tablespoons flour
1 teaspoon vanilla extract

Topping and Assembly

7 tablespoons brown sugar
6 tablespoons flour
2 teaspoons cinnamon
2 tablespoons butter

3 cups fresh blueberries or drained thawed frozen blueberries

For the crust, combine the flour, sugar and salt in a food processor container. Process until mixed. Add the shortening and butter. Pulse until crumbly. Add just enough of the cold water until the mixture adheres, processing constantly. Shape the dough into a ball and wrap loosely in plastic wrap. Flatten into a disk. Chill for 1 to 10 hours.

Roll the dough into a 13-inch circle on a lightly floured surface. Press the dough over the bottom and up the side of an 11-inch tart pan with removable bottom; trim the edge. Chill in the refrigerator.

For the filling, process the almonds and sugar in a food processor until ground. Add the egg, butter, flour and vanilla. Pulse until of the consistency of a thick paste.

For the topping, combine the brown sugar, flour and cinnamon in a bowl and mix well. Cut in the butter until crumbly.

To assemble, spread the filling in the prepared tart pan. Sprinkle with the blueberries and topping. Arrange the tart pan on a baking sheet. Bake at 375 degrees for 1 to 1¹/₂ hours or until the crust is golden brown and the filling is set. Cool slightly on a wire rack. Serve warm or at room temperature with vanilla ice cream.

Yield: 8 to 10 servings

Chocolate Tart with Mixed Nut Crust

From Rancho de San Juan

Nut Crust
1 cup coarsely ground walnuts
1 cup coarsely ground pine nuts
3/4 cup sugar
1/2 cup (1 stick) butter, melted

Chocolate Filling
6 ounces bittersweet chocolate, finely chopped
5 tablespoons unsalted butter
8 egg yolks
1/4 cup sugar
1/2 teaspoon almond extract
1 teaspoon Cognac
6 ounces bittersweet chocolate, coarsely chopped
Whipped cream
Baking cocoa

For the crust, combine the walnuts, pine nuts, sugar and butter in a bowl and mix well. Press the walnut mixture over the bottom and up the side of a 9-inch fluted tart pan with removable bottom. Bake at 350 degrees for 15 minutes. Let stand until cool.

For the filling, combine the finely chopped chocolate and butter in a double boiler over simmering water. Heat just until blended, stirring occasionally. Cool to room temperature. Beat the egg yolks in a mixing bowl until blended. Add the sugar, flavoring and Cognac. Beat at high speed until pale yellow and thick.

Fold the melted chocolate mixture into the egg mixture. Stir in the coarsely chopped chocolate. Spoon into the prepared tart pan. Bake at 300 degrees for 10 to 12 minutes or just until the filling is set and the top is crusty. Let stand until cool. Top each serving with a dollop of whipped cream and sprinkle lightly with baking cocoa.

Yield: 6 to 8 servings

Raspberry and White Chocolate Tart

Crust

3/4 cup cake flour
3/4 cup all-purpose flour
1/4 cup sugar
1/2 cup (1 stick) unsalted butter, cut into pieces, chilled

1 egg yolk
1 tablespoon whipping cream
2 tablespoons (about) cold water

Filling and Assembly

2 cups (12 ounces) white chocolate chips
1/2 cup whipping cream, heated
1/4 cup (1/2 stick) unsalted butter, softened
1/4 cup cake flour
1/4 cup lemon juice

Grated zest of 2 large lemons
2 cups fresh raspberries or drained thawed frozen unsweetened raspberries
Confectioners' sugar
Fresh raspberries
Sprigs of mint

For the crust, combine the cake flour, all-purpose flour and sugar in a bowl and mix well. Cut in the butter until crumbly. Whisk the egg yolk and whipping cream in a bowl until blended. Pour over the flour mixture and stir until the mixture adheres, adding the water to bind the dough. Shape the dough into a ball and flatten into a disk. Chill, wrapped in plastic wrap, for 30 minutes.

Roll the dough 1/8 inch thick on a lightly floured surface. Fit the dough into a 9-inch tart pan with removable bottom; trim the edge. Chill for 30 minutes. Line the dough with foil and fill with dried beans. Bake at 350 degrees for 15 minutes. Remove the beans and foil. Bake for 15 minutes longer or until golden brown. Cool in pan on a wire rack.

For the filling, place the white chocolate chips in a microwave-safe dish. Microwave on Low for 1 minute and stir. Repeat this process until the chocolate is melted. Stir in the whipping cream, butter, cake flour, lemon juice and lemon zest.

To assemble, sprinkle 2 cups raspberries over the baked layer. Pour the white chocolate filling over the raspberries. Chill for 24 hours. Sprinkle lightly with confectioners' sugar. Slice and top each serving with a couple of raspberries and a sprig of mint.

Yield: 8 servings

Chewy Chocolate Gingerbread Cookies

1½ cups plus 1 tablespoon flour
1 tablespoon baking cocoa
1¼ teaspoons ground ginger
1 teaspoon cinnamon
¼ teaspoon ground cloves
¼ teaspoon nutmeg
1 teaspoon baking soda
1½ teaspoons boiling water
½ cup (1 stick) unsalted butter, softened
1 tablespoon grated gingerroot
½ cup packed brown sugar
¼ cup molasses
7 ounces semisweet chocolate chips
¼ cup sugar

Sift the flour, baking cocoa, ground ginger, cinnamon, cloves and nutmeg into a bowl and mix well. Dissolve the baking soda in the boiling water in a small bowl.

Beat the butter and grated gingerroot in a mixing bowl for 4 minutes or until light and fluffy. Add the brown sugar. Beat until blended. Add the molasses. Beat until blended. Add half the flour mixture and beat until smooth. Add the baking soda mixture and remaining flour mixture and beat until blended. Stir in the chocolate chips.

Pat the dough 1 inch thick on a sheet of plastic wrap. Seal in the plastic wrap and chill for 2 hours. Shape the dough into 1-inch balls. Chill for 20 minutes. Roll in the sugar. Arrange the balls 2 inches apart on a cookie sheet. Bake at 325 degrees for 13 to 15 minutes or until light brown. Cool on cookie sheet for 2 minutes. Remove to a wire rack to cool completely.

Yield: 2 dozen cookies

Double-Chocolate Shortbread

From Mia Maes-Blankenau of Until We Eat Again

1¹/4 cups confectioners' sugar
1 cup (2 sticks) unsalted butter, softened
1 tablespoon vanilla extract
¹/2 cup baking cocoa
¹/4 teaspoon salt
2 to 2¹/2 cups flour
1 cup chopped white, milk or dark chocolate, melted

Beat the confectioners' sugar and butter in a mixing bowl until creamy. Add the vanilla and beat until blended. Add the baking cocoa and mix well. Beat in the salt. Add the flour gradually, mixing constantly until a very stiff dough forms. Use your hands if necessary to mix the dough.

Turn the dough onto a hard surface dusted lightly with baking cocoa. Roll ¹/2 inch thick. Cut the dough into desired shapes. Arrange the cookies on a cookie sheet lined with baking parchment. Bake at 350 degrees for 6 to 7 minutes or until crisp around the edges. Cool on cookie sheet for 2 minutes. Remove to a wire rack to cool completely. Drizzle with the melted chocolate.

Yield: 2 dozen cookies

Mia Maes-Blankenau, a native New Mexican, began cooking as a child growing up in Santa Fe and later honed her skills in fine restaurants across the Southwest. Later as head chef and owner of Until We Eat Again, Mia catered for New Mexico's finest for over eight years. Her passions are her family, volunteerism, and of course dark chocolate. She has recently retired from the culinary field.

Gila Monster Cookies

$1^1/2$ cups chunky peanut butter
1 cup sugar
1 cup packed plus 2 tablespoons brown sugar
$^1/2$ cup (1 stick) margarine, softened
3 eggs
2 teaspoons baking soda
$^1/4$ teaspoon vanilla extract
$4^1/4$ cups rolled oats
$1^1/3$ cups (8 ounces) chocolate chips
8 ounces "M & M's" Chocolate Candies
Shredded coconut (optional)
Raisins (optional)

Combine the peanut butter, sugar, brown sugar, margarine, eggs, baking soda and vanilla in a mixing bowl and mix well. Combine the oats, chocolate chips, chocolate candies, coconut and raisins in a bowl and mix well. Add the peanut butter mixture to the oats mixture and mix well.

Drop the dough by $1^1/2$ teaspoonfuls 2 inches apart onto a greased cookie sheet. Bake at 350 degrees for 8 to 10 minutes or until light brown. Cool on cookie sheet for 2 minutes. Remove to a wire rack to cool completely.

Yield: 5 to 6 dozen cookies

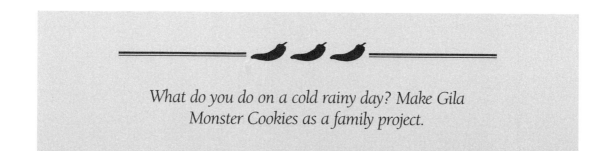

What do you do on a cold rainy day? Make Gila Monster Cookies as a family project.

Santa Fe Chief Sugar Cookies

4¼ cups sifted flour
1 teaspoon baking soda
1 teaspoon cream of tartar
½ teaspoon salt
1 cup (2 sticks) butter, softened
1 cup sugar
2 eggs, beaten
1 teaspoon vanilla extract
1 cup confectioners' sugar, sifted
1 cup vegetable oil
Sugar to taste

Sift the flour, baking soda, cream of tartar and salt into a bowl and mix well. Beat the butter and 1 cup sugar in a mixing bowl until light and fluffy. Beat in the eggs and vanilla until blended. Add the confectioners' sugar 1 tablespoon at a time, mixing well after each addition. Add the oil gradually and beat until blended. Beat in the flour mixture.

Shape the dough into 1-inch balls. Roll in sugar to taste. Arrange the balls 2 inches apart on an ungreased cookie sheet. Flatten the balls to ¼ inch thick with a glass dipped in sugar. Bake at 375 degrees for 10 to 12 minutes or until light brown. Cool on cookie sheet for 2 minutes. Remove to a wire rack to cool completely. Store in an airtight container. May store, covered, in the refrigerator for several weeks. Do not freeze.

Yield: 130 to 150 cookies

My great-grandmother obtained this sugar cookie recipe from the Santa Fe Railroad's dining car chef in the 1930s. It makes the best cookies I have ever tasted. To my knowledge, this recipe has never been published.

Bizcochitos

From Jane Butel

6 cups sifted flour	2 teaspoons anise seeds
1 tablespoon baking powder	2 eggs
1 teaspoon salt	1/4 cup (or more) brandy
1 pound lard or butter	1/4 cup sugar
1 1/2 cups sugar	1 tablespoon cinnamon

Sift the flour, baking powder and salt into a bowl and mix well. Beat the lard, 1 1/2 cups sugar and anise seeds in a mixing bowl at medium speed until creamy, scraping the bowl occasionally. Beat the eggs in a mixing bowl until light and fluffy. Add to the creamed mixture and beat until blended. Add the flour mixture and just enough of the brandy to make a stiff dough and mix well.

Knead the dough lightly on a lightly floured surface. Pat or roll 1/4- to 1/2-inch thick. Cut into desired shapes; the fleur-de-lis shape is traditional for these cookies. Arrange the cookies on a cookie sheet. Sprinkle with a mixture of 1/4 cup sugar and cinnamon. Bake at 350 degrees for 10 minutes or until light brown. Cool on cookie sheet for 2 minutes. Remove to a wire rack to cool completely.

Yield: 5 dozen cookies

Bizcochitos are New Mexico's state cookie. There are various recipes. This one has been passed down in my family for three generations. They are wonderful if you make them with lard, roll about 3/8 inch thick, and are careful with the flour. Do sift or spoon the flour into the measuring cup and do not add much flour when rolling. They are best that way. A special note: Lard is the healthiest of all shortenings, contrary to popular belief. It has less cholesterol and less saturated fat than butter and is an all natural product with no trans fats, etc., such as hydrogenated shortenings. It also is the shortest of all shortenings— producing the most moist and flaky baked goods.

Triple-Chocolate Biscotti

From Mia Maes-Blankenau of Until We Eat Again

1 cup (2 sticks) unsalted butter, softened
4 ounces dark chocolate, finely chopped
2 cups flour
1/2 cup baking cocoa
1 1/2 teaspoons baking powder
1/2 teaspoon salt
1 cup sugar
2 eggs
1 tablespoon vanilla extract
1 cup chopped dark or white chocolate, melted

Combine the butter and 4 ounces dark chocolate in a microwave-safe dish or double boiler. Microwave or heat just until melted and stir to blend. Combine the flour, baking cocoa, baking powder and salt in a bowl and mix well. Beat the sugar and eggs in a mixing bowl until light and fluffy. Beat in the vanilla. Add the melted chocolate mixture and mix until blended. Beat in the flour mixture until smooth.

Shape the dough into 1 large or 2 small logs on a lightly floured surface. Arrange the log or logs on a cookie sheet lined with baking parchment. Bake at 350 degrees for 30 minutes. Remove the log or logs to a wire rack. Let cool for 15 minutes.

Reduce the oven temperature to 275 degrees. Slice each log diagonally into the desired widths. Arrange the slices on the parchment-lined cookie sheet. Bake for 20 minutes longer. Remove to a wire rack to cool.

Dip the cut sides of the biscotti in 1 cup melted chocolate. Let stand until the chocolate is set. Store in an airtight container.

Yield: 1 dozen cookies or 2 dozen petite cookies

Butterscotch Nugget Bars

1 cup crisp rice cereal
1 (2-layer) package yellow cake mix
1/2 cup (1 stick) butter, softened
1/2 cup butterscotch chips
1 egg
8 ounces cream cheese, softened
1/2 cup butterscotch ice cream topping
1/3 cup chopped almonds

Crush the cereal to measure 1/2 cup. Combine the cereal, cake mix and butter in a mixing bowl. Beat at low speed until crumbly. Stir in the butterscotch chips. Reserve 1 cup of the crumb mixture. Add the egg to the remaining crumb mixture and mix well. Press the crumb mixture over the bottom of a greased 9×13-inch baking pan.

Beat the cream cheese and ice cream topping in the same mixing bowl at medium speed until blended. Spread over the prepared layer. Combine the reserved crumb mixture and almonds in a bowl and mix well. Sprinkle over the top. Bake at 350 degrees for 30 to 35 minutes or until light brown. Cool in pan on a wire rack. Cut into bars.

Yield: 3 dozen bars

Crème de Menthe Squares

Crust
1/2 cup (1 stick) butter
1/2 cup baking cocoa
1/2 cup sifted confectioners' sugar
1 egg, beaten
1 teaspoon vanilla extract
2 cups graham cracker crumbs

Filling
1/2 cup (1 stick) butter, melted
1/3 cup crème de menthe
3 cups confectioners' sugar

Topping
1/4 cup (1/2 stick) butter
9 ounces (1 1/2 cups) semisweet chocolate chips

For the crust, combine the butter and baking cocoa in a saucepan over low heat. Cook until blended, stirring frequently. Remove from heat. Stir in the confectioners' sugar, egg and vanilla. Add the graham cracker crumbs and mix well. Press into a 9×13-inch dish.

For the filling, combine the butter and crème de menthe in a mixing bowl and mix well. Add the confectioners' sugar and beat until of a spreading consistency. Spread over the crust. Chill, covered, for 1 hour.

For the topping, heat the butter and chocolate chips in a saucepan until blended, stirring frequently. Spread over the chilled layers. Chill, covered, until set. Cut into squares.

Yield: 3 to 4 dozen squares

Fudgy Raspberry Bars

Bars

10 ounces bittersweet or semisweet chocolate, chopped	1 cup sugar
	5 eggs
3/4 cup (1 1/2 sticks) unsalted butter, cut into pieces	1/3 cup flour
	1 teaspoon baking powder
1/3 cup seedless raspberry jam	

Glaze and Assembly

1/4 cup whipping cream	12 ounces fresh raspberries
1/4 cup seedless raspberry jam	1 cup whipping cream
	1 tablespoon confectioners' sugar
6 ounces bittersweet or semisweet chocolate	1 teaspoon vanilla extract

For the bars, line a 9×9-inch baking pan with foil. Coat the foil with butter and dust lightly with flour. Combine the chocolate and butter in a medium heavy saucepan over low heat. Cook until smooth, stirring frequently. Whisk in the jam. Cook until blended, stirring constantly. Cool slightly. Beat the sugar and eggs in a mixing bowl for 6 minutes or until thickened, scraping the bowl occasionally. Sift the flour and baking powder over the egg mixture and fold in. Fold in the chocolate mixture.

Spoon the batter into the prepared pan. Bake at 350 degrees for 45 minutes or until the top of the cake is slightly crusty and begins to crack and a wooden pick inserted in the center comes out with moist crumbs attached. Cool in pan for 5 minutes. Gently press down any raised edges of the baked layer to make level. Cool completely in the pan on a wire rack. Invert onto a serving platter. Discard the foil and trim 1/2 inch off the edges.

For the glaze, combine 1/4 cup whipping cream and jam in a saucepan over medium heat. Bring to a boil, stirring frequently. Remove from heat. Add the chocolate, stirring until blended. Let stand for 15 minutes or until cool and of a spreadable consistency. Spread over the baked layer.

To assemble, sprinkle with the raspberries. Cut into bars. Beat 1 cup whipping cream in a mixing bowl until soft peaks form. Add the confectioners' sugar and vanilla and mix well. Top each bar with a dollop of the whipped cream.

Yield: 1 dozen bars

Lemon Cheese Squares

1 (2-layer) golden cake mix
1/2 cup (1 stick) butter, melted
1 egg
1/2 cup chopped pecans
2 cups confectioners' sugar
8 ounces cream cheese, softened
1/4 cup sour cream
2 eggs
1 tablespoon grated lemon zest
1 teaspoon vanilla extract

Combine the cake mix, butter and 1 egg in a bowl and mix well. Stir in the pecans. Press the pecan mixture over the bottom of an ungreased 9×13-inch baking dish. Beat the confectioners' sugar, cream cheese and sour cream in a mixing bowl until smooth. Add 2 eggs, lemon zest and vanilla and mix well.

Spread the cream cheese mixture over the prepared layer. Bake at 350 degrees for 30 minutes. Cool in dish on a wire rack. Chill, covered, for 3 hours. Cut into squares. Serve cold.

Yield: 3 to 4 dozen squares

Native American villages along the Rio Grande are called pueblos, a name they received from the early Spanish explorers. Today, many pueblos are open to the public. It's best to call the pueblo or the Indian Cultural Center to clarify its visitors' policy. Remember: When visiting, you are under the laws of the pueblo.

Mí Casa es Su Casa

Authentic Flavors from New Mexico

The Spell of Chimayó

Good Friday marks the pilgrimage to the Santuario de Chimayó. Many Christian pilgrims travel by foot the twenty-seven miles from Santa Fe, and others walk from Albuquerque and elsewhere. Following tradition, pilgrims will often walk barefoot part of the way or crawl the last few yards on their knees.

The story of the Santuario de Chimayó began around 1810 with a Chimayó friar who saw a light bursting from the hillside while he was performing penances. At the lighted spot, he began digging, only to find a crucifix, which became known as the miraculous crucifix of Our Lord of Esquipulas. The crucifix was taken to Santa Cruz, and it disappeared three times, only to be found back in its original hole. The friars took this as a sign that a chapel was to be built on this site. Upon completion of the building, miraculous healings began. These grew so frequent that the chapel was replaced in 1816 by El Santuario de Chimayó shrine, which stands today.

El Santuario has become one of the most-visited churches in New Mexico. The original crucifix still sits on the chapel altar, but many now believe that the pit from which it came has even more significance. More than 300,000 people visit this site every year to take away a bit of sacred dirt from the "sacred sand pit." The walls of the sacristy are covered with discarded crutches and other evidence of healing miracles.

Comin' Home

All Your Favorites that Mama Used to Make

Chile con Queso

Guacamole Salad

Stuffed Green Chiles

Tamales

Spanish Rice

Refried Beans

Classic Mexican Flan

These classic favorites need only an assortment of tortillas—
both crispy and soft.

Chile Pronto

When You Don't Have the Time to Cook Like Mama

Southwestern Cobb Salad

Northern New Mexico-Style Stuffed Green Chiles

Spicy Green Chile Sauce or Gringo Red Chile Sauce

Spanish Rice

Velarde Apple Cake

If you've got 5 more minutes, throw in the guacamole and chips.

Chile con Queso

From Jane Butel

1/3 cup vegetable oil
1/2 cup finely chopped onion, or 3 green onions, chopped
1 garlic clove, finely minced
1 tablespoon flour
3/4 cup evaporated milk
1 tomato, chopped
3 tablespoons finely minced jalapeño chiles
1 pound processed cheese, cut into 1-inch cubes
1/2 cup mixed shredded Monterey Jack cheese and Cheddar cheese

Heat the oil in a heavy saucepan. Add the onion and garlic. Sauté until onion is tender. Stir in the flour. Stir in the evaporated milk gradually. Cook until mixture thickens slightly, stirring constantly.

Add the tomato, jalapeño chiles, processed cheese, Monterey Jack and Cheddar cheeses. Cook for 5 minutes or until thickened and smooth, stirring constantly.

This may be kept warm in a chafing dish over hot, not boiling, water. Leftover Chile con Queso is excellent on hamburgers, used in omelets or spooned over crisp tortillas for instant nachos.

Yield: 2 cups

Literally translated, this is chile with cheese, and it is the Southwest's most popular hot dip. Serve warm with tortilla chips. Chile con queso may be poured into a rigid container and frozen up to four months.

Gringo Red Chile Sauce

1 garlic clove, minced
3 tablespoons olive oil
2 tablespoons flour

¹/₂ cup BUENO® chile powder
2 cups water
Salt to taste

Sauté the garlic in the olive oil in a saucepan. Stir in the flour. Stir in the chile powder. Whisk in the water. Cook until of the desired consistency, stirring constantly. Season with salt.

Yield: 2 cups

Red Chile Sauce

16 to 18 BUENO® dried
red chile pods

2 garlic cloves
Salt to taste

Cut each chile pod open. Rinse and remove any blemishes. Discard the stems and some of the seeds. Discard enough veins to make of the desired taste; the more veins used the hotter the chile sauce will be. Rinse with cold water. Place in a bowl. Add enough hot water to cover. Let stand for 1 hour or until chiles are soft; drain. Place in a blender container. Add enough water to almost cover the chiles. Process for 2 to 3 minutes or until smooth and skins are not visible, adding additional water as needed. Add the garlic and process until smooth. Season with salt.

Yield: Variable

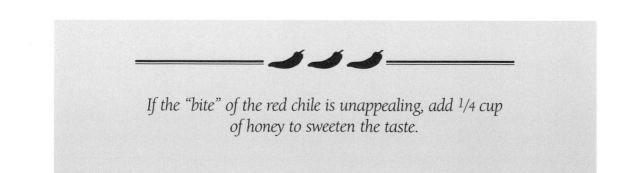

If the "bite" of the red chile is unappealing, add ¹/₄ cup of honey to sweeten the taste.

Spicy Green Chile Sauce

1 garlic clove (optional)
1/2 cup minced onion (optional)
2 tablespoons vegetable oil or lard
1 tablespoon flour
1 cup water
1 cup BUENO® frozen green chile
Salt to taste

Sauté the garlic and onion in the oil in a saucepan. Stir in the flour. Whisk in the water. Add the green chile. Bring to a boil, stirring constantly. Reduce the heat. Simmer for 5 minutes, stirring frequently. Season with salt. This sauce may be used as a topping for eggs, served with beans or meat, used in tacos or made into green enchiladas.

Yield: 1 1/2 cups

Salsa Supreme

1 large tomato, chopped
1 onion, chopped
1/2 cup BUENO® frozen green chile, drained
1/2 teaspoon garlic salt
Salt to taste

Combine the tomato, onion, green chile and garlic salt in a bowl and mix well. Season with salt. Chill, covered, for 1 hour or longer.

Yield: 2 cups

Stuffed Green Chiles
Chiles Rellenos

1 cup flour
1 teaspoon baking powder
$^1/_2$ teaspoon salt
$^3/_4$ cup cornmeal
1 cup milk
2 eggs, beaten
10 ounces longhorn or Monterey Jack cheese
10 whole BUENO® frozen green chiles, thawed
Oil for frying

Combine the flour, baking powder, salt and cornmeal in a bowl and mix well. Combine the milk and eggs in a bowl and mix well. Pour into the dry ingredients, stirring until smooth and adding additional milk if needed. Cut the cheese into 10 slices $^1/_2$-inch thick and the length of the chiles.

Make a small slit in the top of each chile. Insert a slice of cheese into each chile. Dip the chiles in the batter to coat. Cook in hot oil in a skillet until golden brown on all sides. Set on paper towels to drain. You may serve with Spicy Green Chile Sauce if desired.

Yield: 5 servings

Guacamole Salad

5 large avocados
1 garlic clove, minced
2½ teaspoons lemon juice
1 teaspoon salt
1 tomato, seeded, chopped

1 small jalapeño chile, seeded, finely minced
Whole or shredded lettuce leaves
Chopped tomato

Peel and chop the avocados. Place in a bowl and mash. Add the garlic, lemon juice, salt, tomato, and jalapeño chile and mix well. Arrange the lettuce leaves over 4 salad plates. Spoon the guacamole evenly over the lettuce. Garnish with chopped tomato. Serve with tostados.

Yield: 4 servings

Tortilla Soup

1 onion, chopped
2 cups chopped cooked potatoes
2 garlic cloves, minced
8 cups chicken broth

1 envelope taco seasoning mix
6 cups chopped cooked chicken
1 (28-ounce) can diced tomatoes

Combine the onion, potatoes, garlic and broth in a saucepan. Bring to a simmer. Simmer until the onion is tender. Stir in the taco seasoning. Add the chicken and tomatoes and mix well. Simmer for 10 minutes. Spoon into soup bowls or hollowed out miniature gourds or squash. Garnish with shredded cheese, chopped cilantro, chopped green onions, chopped tomatoes, a dollop of sour cream, fresh lime juice, lime wedges or toasted tortilla chips.

Yield: 8 servings

Isleta Bread

From PNM's Cocinas de New Mexico

1 envelope dry yeast
$1/4$ cup warm (105- to 115-degree) water
$1/2$ teaspoon shortening
$1/4$ teaspoon honey
$1/4$ teaspoon salt
1 cup hot water
5 cups (about) flour

Dissolve the yeast in $1/4$ cup warm water in a small bowl. Combine the shortening, honey, salt and 1 cup hot water in a large bowl. Stir until shortening is dissolved. Let stand until room temperature. Stir in the yeast mixture. Add enough flour to make a moderately firm dough. Knead on a floured surface until smooth and elastic. Place in a greased bowl, turning to coat the surface. Let rise, covered, in a warm place until doubled in bulk. Punch the dough down. Knead on a floured surface. Place in the greased bowl. Let rise until doubled in bulk.

Divide dough into two equal parts. Shape each half into a flat 8-inch diameter circle. Fold each circle almost in half, allowing the bottom half to extend beyond the top half by 1 inch. Cut the dough, from the folded edge towards the opposite edge, twice, dividing the loaf partially into thirds. Arrange the dough into two greased 9-inch pie plates, separating the cuts and creating a crescent effect. Let rise until doubled in bulk.

Place a shallow pan of water on the bottom oven rack. Place the loaves in the oven so that neither is directly above the water. Bake at 350 degrees for 1 hour.

Yield: 2 loaves

Deep-Fried Bread
Sopaipillas

From Jane Butel

4 cups flour	1/4 cup warm (105- to
1 1/2 teaspoons salt	115-degree) water
1 teaspoon baking	1 1/4 cups (about) scalded
powder	milk, cooled to room
1 tablespoon lard or butter	temperature
1 envelope dry yeast	Oil for deep-frying

Combine the flour, salt and baking powder in a bowl and mix well. Cut in the lard until crumbly. Dissolve the yeast in the warm water. Stir into the cooled scalded milk. Add 1 1/4 cups of the liquid to the dry ingredients stirring to form a dough. Add enough of the remaining 1/4 cup liquid gradually to make a dough that is firm and holds its shape. Knead the dough on a floured surface for 5 minutes or until smooth and elastic. Invert the bowl over the dough. Let rest for 10 minutes or until dough will yield a hole when poked. Pour the oil into a deep fryer to a depth of 3 to 4 inches. Heat to 400 degrees.

Divide the dough into 4 equal portions. Roll 1 portion 1/4 inch thick or slightly thinner, keeping the remaining portions covered with plastic wrap. Cut the rolled dough into triangles or squares; do not reroll any of the dough. Fry the sopaipillas, in batches, in the hot oil until puffed and hollow; holding under the surface of the oil if needed. Repeat with the remaining portions of dough. You may omit the yeast and water and increase the milk to 1 1/2 cups.

Yield: 4 dozen

Sopaipillas are truly native to New Mexico, originating in Old Town, Albuquerque, over three hundred years ago. These hollow puffs can be served as a bread and torn apart to layer with honey. They are delicious sprinkled with cinnamon and sugar as a dessert or snack and make wonderful "pocket bread" for stuffing with refried beans, chile con carne, and sauces for a main dish sandwich.

Refried Beans
Frijoles Refritos

3 tablespoons lard or bacon drippings
2 cups cooked pinto beans
1/2 cup shredded longhorn cheese

Heat the lard in a skillet. Add the beans and mash. Simmer for 5 minutes. Sprinkle the cheese over the top. Cook until cheese is melted.

Yield: 6 servings

New Mexico Pinto Beans

3 cups dried pinto beans
10 cups hot water
1 meaty ham bone, or 4 ounces salt pork or cubed bacon
1 teaspoon salt, or to taste

Rinse the beans, discarding any loose skins or shriveled beans. Place in a large pot with a lid. Cover with the hot water. Let stand, covered, for 8 to 12 hours. Bring to a simmer. Add the ham bone. Cook, covered, until beans are tender, adding additional hot or boiling water as needed; beans will turn dark if cold water is added or if cooked uncovered. Season with salt. Let stand before serving.

Yield: 8 to 12 servings

Calabacitas

3 or 4 zucchini or yellow squash, sliced
1 large onion, chopped
3 tablespoons vegetable oil
1/4 teaspoon garlic salt, or
2 garlic cloves, minced
1/2 cup BUENO® frozen green chile, drained
1 (16-ounce) can whole kernel corn
1 cup shredded Cheddar cheese

Sauté the zucchini and onion in the oil in a skillet just until tender. Add the garlic salt, green chile, corn and cheese and mix well. Spoon into a buttered 1-quart baking dish. Bake at 400 degrees for 20 minutes.

Yield: 6 servings

Spanish Rice

3 tablespoons shortening
1 1/2 cups rice
1/2 cup sliced onion
1/2 cup sliced bell pepper
1 (14-ounce) can whole tomatoes
1 garlic clove, minced or crushed
1 teaspoon pepper
1 1/2 cups (about) warm water
2 teaspoons salt
1 1/2 cups cold water

Heat the shortening in a large skillet until melted. Add the rice and cook until brown. Reduce the heat. Add the onion, bell pepper, tomatoes, garlic and pepper and mix well. Stir in enough of the warm water to cover the rice. Stir in the salt. Bring to a simmer. Simmer, covered, until almost all liquid is absorbed. Reduce the heat to low. Add the cold water gradually until rice is fluffy.

Yield: 4 to 6 servings

New Mexican Green Chile Stew
Caldillo

2 pounds lean round
steak or pork
Salt to taste
2 tablespoons vegetable oil
3 potatoes, peeled, chopped

1/2 cup sliced onion
1 large garlic clove, minced
2 teaspoons salt
3/4 cup BUENO® frozen
green chile

Cut the steak into bite-size pieces. Sprinkle with salt to taste. Heat the oil in a skillet until hot. Add the steak and cook until brown. Add the potatoes, onion, garlic, 2 teaspoons salt and enough green chile to make of the desired taste. Add enough water to cover. Cook until meat and potatoes are tender, adding additional water if needed; stew should have a soupy consistency.

Yield: 4 servings

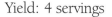

Beef Tacos

1 pound ground beef
1 onion, chopped
Salt to taste
1 garlic clove, minced
(optional)
12 taco shells

Shredded lettuce
1 tomato, chopped
Shredded Cheddar cheese
1 cup Spicy Green Chile
Sauce or Salsa Supreme
(page 195)

Brown the ground beef with the onion in a skillet until beef is crumbly; drain. Season with salt. Stir in the garlic. Place a heaping tablespoon of the beef mixture in each taco shell. Layer the lettuce, tomato and cheese over the beef mixture. Serve with Spicy Green Chile Sauce or Salsa Supreme.

Yield: 6 servings

Chalupas

1 pound ground beef
Oil for frying
6 BUENO® corn tortillas
1 cup refried beans
Salsa to taste
1 garlic clove, minced
$1/2$ cup minced onion
1 cup shredded Cheddar cheese
$1^1/2$ cups shredded lettuce
1 tomato, chopped
$1^1/2$ cups guacamole
$1/2$ cup sour cream
Sliced olives

Brown the ground beef in a skillet, stirring until crumbly; drain. Heat the oil in a separate skillet. Cook the tortillas in the hot oil, 1 at a time, pressing down in the center to form a cup-shape. Drain on paper towels.

Combine the beans and salsa in a bowl and mix well. Spoon into the cup-shaped tortillas. Spoon the cooked ground beef over the bean mixture. Sprinkle with the garlic, onion and cheese. Place on a baking sheet. Bake at 375 degrees for 10 minutes.

Sprinkle the lettuce over the hot chalupas. Spoon the tomato and guacamole over the lettuce. Top with a dollop of sour cream. Garnish with olives.

Yield: 6 servings

Northern New Mexico-Style Stuffed Green Chiles

Chiles Rellenos Norte Nuevo Mexicanos

From PNM's Cocinas de New Mexico

8 ounces lean ground beef
1/4 cup finely chopped onion
2 tablespoons flour
1 1/2 cups beef bouillon
3/4 teaspoon salt
1/4 teaspoon garlic powder
1/4 teaspoon oregano
1/4 teaspoon cumin
1 cup BUENO® frozen green chile, or to taste
4 eggs, beaten
4 whole BUENO® frozen green chiles, cut into halves
4 ounces sharp Cheddar cheese, shredded

Brown the ground beef with the onion in a skillet over medium heat, stirring until beef is crumbly; drain. Stir in the flour. Add the bouillon, salt, garlic powder, oregano and cumin and mix well. Cook until the sauce begins to thicken, stirring constantly. Stir in the chopped green chile. Simmer for 15 minutes.

Heat a small skillet coated with nonstick cooking spray until hot. Add the eggs. Cook until of the desired consistency, stirring constantly.

Divide the eggs evenly among 4 plates. Place 2 chile halves over the eggs on each plate. Spoon the sauce over the chiles. Sprinkle the cheese over the top. You may place the plates in a 350-degree oven and bake until the cheese is melted.

Yield: 4 servings

Meat Turnovers
Empanaditas de Carne

1 pound beef chuck
1 pound lean pork
1 cup raisins
2 cups applesauce or mincemeat, or 1 cup applesauce and 1 cup mincemeat
1 cup sugar
1 teaspoon cinnamon
1/2 teaspoon cloves
1 teaspoon salt
1/2 cup piñon nuts or chopped pecans
3 cups flour
1 tablespoon sugar
1 teaspoon baking powder
1 teaspoon salt
3 tablespoons shortening or lard
1 egg, beaten
1 cup water
Oil for frying

Combine the beef with enough water to cover in a saucepan. Bring to a boil. Reduce the heat. Simmer until tender. Drain, reserving the broth. Combine the pork with enough water to cover in a saucepan. Bring to a boil. Reduce the heat. Simmer until tender. Drain, reserving the broth. Grind the beef and pork.

Combine the ground beef, ground pork, raisins, applesauce, 1 cup sugar, cinnamon, cloves, salt and piñon nuts in a large stockpot and mix well. Stir in enough of the reserved broths to moisten thoroughly. Bring to a simmer. Simmer for 15 minutes. Stir in additional broth if mixture is too dry. Let stand until cool.

Combine the flour, 1 tablespoon sugar, baking powder and salt in a bowl and mix well. Cut in the shortening until crumbly. Stir in the egg. Add the water gradually, mixing until the mixture forms a ball. Roll 1/8 inch thick on a lightly floured surface. Cut with a biscuit cutter. Fill each round with the meat mixture. Fold the dough over and pinch to seal the edge. Deep-fry the turnovers, in batches, in hot oil until browned.

Yield: 36 turnovers

Marinated Pork
Carne Adovada

4 pounds pork, such as spareribs or shoulder chops
2 teaspoons salt
3 garlic cloves
2 to 3 teaspoons whole leaf oregano
4 cups Red Chile Sauce (page 194)

Place the pork in a shallow dish. Sprinkle the salt over the pork. Combine the garlic, oregano and Red Chile Sauce. Sprinkle over the pork. Marinate, covered in the refrigerator, for 6 to 12 hours. Place the pork in a Dutch oven. Cook over low heat or bake at 350 degrees for 1 hour or until the pork is tender. You may marinate thick slices of potatoes with the pork if desired.

Yield: 6 servings

The "ristras" which decorate New Mexico's countryside in the fall are strings of red chiles sun-drying for preservation and later use in sauces. The stems are always removed and the seeds may be removed for a milder flavor.

Tamales

From Bueno Foods

2 packages BUENO® cornhusks	4 garlic cloves, minced, or
3¹/2 pounds lean	2 teaspoons garlic powder
boneless pork	3 cups lard or shortening
28 BUENO® chile pods	5 pounds BUENO® masa
2 teaspoons salt, or to taste	1 tablespoon baking powder
1 teaspoon crushed oregano	5 teaspoons salt

Soak the cornhusks with enough hot water to cover in a large bowl until pliable; drain. Combine the pork with enough water to cover in a large saucepan. Bring to a boil. Reduce the heat. Simmer until tender. Drain, reserving the broth. Shred the pork.

Remove the stems and seeds from the chile pods. Rinse the chile pods. Combine with enough water to cover in a saucepan. Boil for 15 minutes or until soft. Drain, reserving the liquid. Purée the chile pods, 5 cups of the reserved chile liquid, 2 teaspoons salt, oregano and garlic in a blender.

Combine the shredded pork and 5 cups of the chile purée in a saucepan. Cook for 10 minutes, stirring frequently.

Beat the lard in a mixing bowl until fluffy. Add the masa and mix well. Add the baking powder and 5 teaspoons salt and mix well. Knead in 3 cups of the reserved pork broth until light and creamy. Spread ¹/8 to ¹/4 inch thick over the prepared cornhusks. Spread ¹/4 cup of the meat mixture over the masa mixture. Fold the longest sides towards the center. Fold the remaining sides towards the center and secure with a cornhusk strip. Steam the tamales for 1 to 1¹/2 hours; do not allow water to touch the tamales.

Yield: 5 dozen tamales

One simply cannot experience Southwestern cuisine without its crowning glory, the tamale. Humble in its beginnings but world-renowned in its flavor, BUENO® Foods shares their timeless and authentic recipe for your enjoyment.

Chicken-Filled Fried Tortillas
Chimichangas de Pollo

From PNM's Cocinas de New Mexico

1 onion
2 cloves
1 (3¹/₂-pound) chicken
6 cups water
2 celery ribs
2 large garlic cloves
1 bay leaf
1 large onion, thinly sliced
1 garlic clove, minced
2 tablespoons shortening
1 large tomato, chopped
1 jalapeño chile, chopped, or to taste
1 teaspoon salt

¹/₈ teaspoon pepper
¹/₄ teaspoon crushed oregano
¹/₄ teaspoon crushed basil
¹/₈ teaspoon cinnamon
8 BUENO® flour tortillas, warmed
Shortening
2 cups sour cream (optional)
1 cup guacamole (optional)
2 cups shredded Cheddar cheese (optional)
Shredded lettuce (optional)
Tomato wedges (optional)

Stud the whole onion with the cloves. Combine with the chicken, water, celery, 2 garlic cloves and bay leaf in a large pot. Cook over medium heat for 1¹/₂ hours or until the chicken is tender; drain. Let chicken stand until cooled. Chop the chicken, discarding the meat and bones.

Sauté the sliced onion and minced garlic in 2 tablespoons shortening in a skillet over medium heat until onion is tender. Add the chicken, tomato, jalapeño chile, salt, pepper, oregano, basil and cinnamon and mix well. Simmer over low heat for 10 to 15 minutes.

Spread about ¹/₂ cup of the chicken mixture horizontally across the bottom half of each tortilla to within 1¹/₂ inches of the edge. Fold the sides in over the filling. Roll as for a jelly roll. Secure with a wooden pick.

Place enough shortening to measure 2 inches deep in a heavy pan. Heat over medium-high heat until hot. Cook each rolled tortilla in the hot shortening until crisp and light brown. Drain on paper towels. Place each chimichanga on a plate. Layer with ¹/₄ cup sour cream, 2 tablespoons guacamole, ¹/₄ cup cheese, lettuce and the tomato wedges.

Yield: 8 servings

Posole

4 cups BUENO® frozen posole, thawed
10 cups water
2 large onions, chopped
4 garlic cloves, finely chopped
2 tablespoons vegetable oil
8 or 9 cups chicken stock
1 teaspoon dried cilantro, or 1 tablespoon chopped fresh cilantro
2 bay leaves
2 tablespoons BUENO® red chile sauce
1 teaspoon Mexican oregano
2 pounds pork roast or chops

Rinse and drain the posole twice. Combine with the water in a saucepan. Cook, covered, for 2 hours or until the posole kernels pop; drain. Rinse the posole; drain.

Sauté the onions and garlic in the oil in a saucepan for 6 to 8 minutes or until onions are tender. Add the posole, 8 cups of the chicken stock, cilantro, bay leaves, red chile sauce and oregano. Cut the pork into 1/2-inch or smaller pieces. Add to the posole mixture. Simmer, covered, for 2 to 3 hours, adding the remaining 1 cup stock if a thinner consistency is desired. Discard bay leaves.

Yield: 8 to 10 servings

Green Chile Sour Cream Enchiladas

From PNM's Cocinas de New Mexico

3 cups chicken broth
3 tablespoons flour
1 cup chopped cooked chicken
1 cup BUENO® frozen green chile, thawed, drained
1/2 teaspoon garlic salt

Shortening
9 BUENO® corn tortillas
2 cups shredded sharp Cheddar cheese
1 onion, chopped
2 cups sour cream

Whisk 1 cup of the broth with the flour in a saucepan until smooth. Whisk in remaining 2 cups broth. Cook over medium heat until thickened, stirring constantly. Stir in the chicken, green chile and garlic salt. Remove from heat. Heat enough shortening in a heavy pan to measure 1/2 inch deep. Soften each tortilla in the shortening. Drain on paper towels. Mix 1 cup of the cheese, onion and sour cream in a bowl. Layer 1/4 cup of the chicken mixture, 1 tortilla, 1/4 cup of the chicken mixture and 1/3 cup of the sour cream mixture 3 times on an ovenproof-dinner plate. Repeat with the remaining ingredients. Top with any remaining chicken mixture. Sprinkle with remaining cheese. Bake at 350 degrees for 15 minutes or until the cheese melts.

Yield: 3 servings

Green Chile Sauce

2/3 cup chopped onion
1 tablespoon butter, lard or bacon drippings
2 tablespoons flour
1 1/2 cups chicken broth

1 cup chopped green chiles
1 cup chopped cooked chicken
1 large garlic clove, minced
3/4 teaspoon salt
Dash of cumin

Sauté the onion in the butter in a saucepan until tender. Stir in the flour. Whisk in the broth. Add the remaining ingredients. Simmer for 20 minutes, stirring frequently.

Green Chile Chicken Enchiladas

From Jane Butel

Oil for frying	Green Chile Sauce (page 210)
8 to 12 white, yellow or blue corn tortillas	1 onion, chopped
	1/4 cup sour cream
6 tablespoons shredded Cheddar cheese	Caribe
	Coarsely chopped lettuce
6 tablespoons shredded Monterey Jack cheese	for garnish
	Tomato wedges for garnish

Heat the oil in a skillet until hot. Fry the tortillas lightly in the oil. Warm 4 ovenproof plates in the oven.

Combine the Cheddar cheese and Monterey Jack cheese in a bowl and mix well. Set aside a small amount of the Green Chile Sauce and a small amount of the cheese. Spread a spoonful of Green Chile Sauce over each warm plate. Layer a tortilla, 1/8 of the cheese, 1/8 of the onion and 1/8 of the remaining Green Chile Sauce twice over the Green Chile Sauce. Top with the reserved Green Chile Sauce and cheeses. Bake at 350 degrees until the cheese melts. Top with a dollop of sour cream and a few grains of caribe. Encircle each enchilada with lettuce and tomato wedges. You may dip the tortillas in chile water or warm in the oven instead of frying.

Rolled Enchiladas: Dip each lightly cooked tortilla in Green Chile Sauce. Sprinkle the cheeses and onion down the center. Roll to enclose the filling. Spoon Green Chile Sauce over the enchiladas and sprinkle with cheese.

Enchiladas for a Crowd: Dip each lightly cooked tortilla in Green Chile Sauce. Sprinkle the cheeses and onion down the center. Roll to enclose the filling. Place in a large shallow baking dish. Bake at 350 degrees until heated through. Heat the Green Chile Sauce in a saucepan. Spoon over the enchiladas. Sprinkle with cheese. Bake until cheese melts. Garnish with lettuce.

Yield: 4 servings

Blue Corn Enchiladas

Oil for frying
12 BUENO® blue corn
tortillas or corn tortillas
1/4 cup vegetable oil or lard
1 garlic clove
1 tablespoon flour

4 cups Spicy Green Chile
Sauce (page 195)
Salt to taste
2 cups shredded Cheddar or
Monterey Jack cheese
1/4 cup minced onion

Heat the oil for frying in a skillet. Fry the tortillas until soft. Drain on paper towels. Heat 1/4 cup oil and garlic in a skillet. Discard the garlic. Stir in the flour. Stir in the Spicy Green Chile Sauce. Cook until heated through, adding water to make of the desired consistency. Season with salt. Set aside a small amount of the cheese. Layer the tortillas, sauce, onion and cheese on 4 ovenproof plates until all of the ingredients are used. Sprinkle the reserved cheese over the top. Bake at 350 degrees until the cheese is melted.

Yield: 4 servings

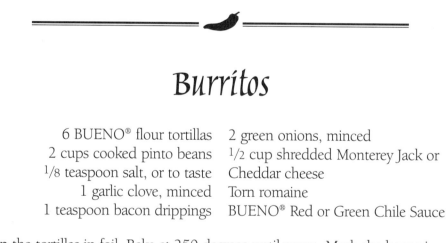

Burritos

6 BUENO® flour tortillas
2 cups cooked pinto beans
1/8 teaspoon salt, or to taste
1 garlic clove, minced
1 teaspoon bacon drippings

2 green onions, minced
1/2 cup shredded Monterey Jack or
Cheddar cheese
Torn romaine
BUENO® Red or Green Chile Sauce

Wrap the tortillas in foil. Bake at 250 degrees until warm. Mash the beans in a bowl. Stir in the salt and garlic. Heat the bacon drippings in a skillet. Add the beans. Cook until heated through, stirring frequently. Spoon down the center of each tortilla. Sprinkle the green onions and cheese over the beans. Roll to enclose the filling. Place on a baking sheet. Bake at 350 degrees for 15 minutes or until cheese is melted. Place each burrito on a plate. Nestle the lettuce around the burritos. Serve with a generous portion of red or green chile sauce. You may substitute a beef, pork or chicken filling for the bean filling.

Yield: 6 servings

Classic Mexican Flan

^{1}/2 cup sugar   3 eggs
1 (14-ounce) can sweetened   3 egg yolks
condensed milk ^{1}/2 teaspoon almond extract
1 cup milk   1 teaspoon vanilla extract

Heat the sugar in a small saucepan over medium heat until it is a dark, caramel-colored liquid, stirring frequently. Remove from the heat. Pour into a 4-cup metal ring mold or 8 individual molds. Swirl to coat the bottom and sides with the caramel. Let stand until caramel hardens. Process the condensed milk, milk, eggs, egg yolks, almond extract and vanilla extract in a blender until well mixed. Pour into the prepared mold. Place the mold in a larger baking pan. Add water to the larger pan to a depth of ^{1}/2 inch. Bake in a preheated 325-degree oven for 1 hour. Remove the mold from the water bath. Let stand until cooled. Chill, covered, for up to 2 days. Invert mold onto a serving plate.

Yield: 8 servings

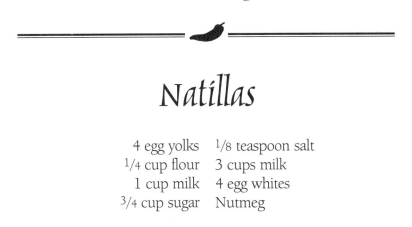

Natillas

4 egg yolks ^{1}/8 teaspoon salt
^{1}/4 cup flour   3 cups milk
1 cup milk   4 egg whites
^{3}/4 cup sugar   Nutmeg

Combine the egg yolks, flour and 1 cup milk in a bowl, stirring until smooth. Combine the sugar, salt and 3 cups milk in a saucepan. Cook until milk is scalded. Stir a small amount of the hot mixture into the egg yolk mixture. Stir the egg yolk mixture into the hot mixture. Cook over medium heat until thickened, stirring constantly. Remove from the heat. Let stand until room temperature. Beat the egg whites in a mixing bowl until stiff peaks form. Fold into the custard. Chill, covered, until ready to serve. Spoon into individual dessert dishes. Sprinkle with nutmeg.

Yield: 6 to 8 servings

Mexican Wedding Cookies

1 cup (2 sticks) butter, softened
1 cup confectioners' sugar
2 cups sifted flour
1 cup ground nuts
1 teaspoon vanilla extract
Confectioners' sugar for coating

Beat the butter, 1 cup confectioners' sugar, flour, nuts and vanilla together in a mixing bowl. Shape into 1½-inch balls. Place on a cookie sheet. Bake at 350 degrees for 10 to 15 minutes or until set. Roll in confectioners' sugar to coat.

Yield: 36 cookies

Dried Red Chile Pods

Red chile pods, stems removed

Rinse and pat dry the chile pods. Remove the seeds if desired. Place the chile pods on a baking sheet. Bake at 250 degrees for 10 minutes, turning several times to prevent scorching.

Red Chile Powder

16 dried red chile pods, stems removed

Process the chile pods, 2 or 3 at a time, in a blender on low speed until finely ground.

Contributors

Restaurants

The Albuquerque Petroleum Club	Albuquerque
The Artichoke Café	Albuquerque
The Bishop's Lodge	Santa Fe
Bueno Foods	Albuquerque
Casa Vieja	Albuquerque
Coyote Café	Santa Fe
Doc Martin's at The Historic Taos Inn	Taos
Double Eagle Restaurant	Historic Old Mesilla
The Old House	Santa Fe
The Pink Adobe	Santa Fe
The Ranchers Club	Albuquerque
Rancho de San Juan	Espanola
Seasons Rotisserie & Grill	Albuquerque
Terra American Bistro	Albuquerque
Tinnie Mercantile Store & Deli	Roswell
Until We Eat Again	Albuquerque
Vista Clara Ranch Resort & Spa	Galisteo

Bed and Breakfast Inns

Casa del Granjero "The Farmer's House"	Albuquerque
Cinnamon Morning Bed & Breakfast	Albuquerque
Hacienda Vargas Bed & Breakfast Inn & Chapel	Algodones
Los Poblanos Inn	Albuquerque
Yours Truly Bed & Breakfast	Corrales

Special Thanks to

Jane Butel of the Jane Butel's Cooking School
Martin Rios of The Old House
Jim White of Casa Vieja

Cocinas de New Mexico
PNM Public Service Company of New Mexico

Contributors

Abbott, Cris
Abraham, Betsy
Alrick, Doris
Alvidrez, Janice
Armayor, Jane
Ashcraft, Melinda
Badger, Amy
Baldwin, Carol
Baldwin, Joan
Baldwin, Tracy
Barkocy, Joyce
Barkoff, Karen
Barnhill, Shannon
Batsel, Margaret
Beach, Alex
Bennett, Lori
Berlin, Becky
Bither, Connie
Bither, Jennifer
Blaugrund, Nancy
Blottner, Myra
Blottner-Elliott, Laura
Bonner, Patsy
Borgeson, Barbara
Brenner, Anne
Brewer, Patricia
Browning, Melinda
Burch, Dixie
Burch, Val
Burks, Janet
Busbey, Diana
Butel, Jane
Byrd, Jennifer
Campbell, Amy
Carter, Tommie

Chalem, Natalie
Chreist, Judy
Christensen, Carole
Churchill, Carole
Clausen, Bonnie
Cline, Ellen
Conran, Catherine
Daniels, Mary
Danz, Elizabeth
Dardanes, Cecelia
Darling, Judy
Darling, Megan
Darling, Susan
Dautel, Cindy
David, Barbara
David, Kristine
Dimmler, Pamela
Douglas, Linda
Douglas, Mike
Dunphy, Janice
Ely, Katy
Federici, Kim
Fereres, Laura
Fickel, Sue
Filyk, Marci
Fischer, Janis
Fitzgerald, Jamie
Fitzgerald, Patty
Franco, Jodi
Frassanito, Elaine
Funke, Dorothy
Gamble, Julie
Giles, Eugenia
Glodt-Stern, Susan
Goldenberg, Kathy

Goldstein, Stacy
Goodman, Martha
Gordon, Paula
Gray, Stefania
Griffith, Karen
Grossetete, Ginger
Hagen, Carol
Hagen-Archer, Heather
Hamill, Jane
Hamrick, Jeanne
Harmon, Karen
Harris, Maybelle
Hartzell, Linda
Harvey, Dusty
Hauptmann, Jan
Hay, Margaret
Hemphill, Billie
Henderson, Carol
Herring, Nancy
Howe, Christine
Howse, Sarah Nelson
Huarte, Susan
Jaramillo, Greg
Johnson, Connie
Jorgensen, Shirley
Kaisersatt, Jane
Kalb, Patricia
Kelly, Marianne
Kenny, Rebecca
Kern, Marnie
Key, Nancy
Knorra, Jill
Knox, Penny
Komoll, Kathy
Lamont, Charlotte

Laskey, Brook
Latimer, Sandra
Lee, Robin
Leonard, Valerie
Letherer, Crissi
Levy, Lisa
Loutfy, Judy
Lynch, Karen
Maccabe, Linda
Macnish, Eleanore
Macnish, Harriette
Maes-Blankenau, Mia
Mager, Lisa
Mallory, Stephanie
Marberry, Phyllis
Martin, Lynn
Martinez, Monica
Martinez, Rachel
Mason, Cre
Mathis, Sara
Mattson, Bethany
McClain-Foltz, Whitney
McClarren, Joyce
McCracken, Jill
McIntosh, Jeanne
McKenzer, Mary
McKinnon, Betty
McMinn, Barbara
McWilliams, Sue
Meister, Meg
Midkiff, Tobie
Minetos, Elizabeth
Mitchell-Lawrence, Kelly
Moore, Sara
Moye, Laurie

Mueller, Lydia
Mulcahy, Diane
Mulverhill-Cole, Jean
Murdock, Barbara
Ogawa, Diane Harrison
Olivas, Caroline
Papiernik, Cheryl
Parsons, Joan
Pate, Becky
Peirce, Letitia
Peppard, Debra Totten
Peterson, Eric
Pierotti, Dinah
Pond, Carol
Pond, Jami
Pratt, Carolyn
Preston, Jo Ann
Raskob, Kathleen
Reardon, Pamela
Redding, Cheryl
Rembe, Penny
Richter, Bobbi
Rivenbark, Ginger
Robinson, Lisa
Rogers, Julie
Root, Bonnie
Rosenstein, Beth
Rost, Eleanore
Sanderson, Amy
Saxton-Fraley, Linda
Schultz, Betsy
Schalk, Dulcie
Sciorilli, Lisa
Shaughnessy, Kate
Sherwood, Maxine

Shubert, Sara
Sington, Cheryl
Sleicher, Sean
Smith, Jean
Stark, Marilyn
Stern, Susan
Stinchcomb, Ann
Stofac, Annie
Stolp, JoAnn
Stolp, Pam
Stolp, Reba Darr
Strange, Kim
Stretz, Sarah
Strong, JoLynn
Strong, Suzanne
Sullivan, Cori
Sullivan, Kay
Thornhill, Joy
Thornton, Betty
Thrall, Debra
Thurston, Irene
Tigert, Sheila
Totten, Lupe
Trail, Connie
Travelstead, Ann
Urrea, Annabell
Utrata, Jennie
von Boetticher, Leigh
Wall, Betty
Webb, Tomai
Wenk, Russ
Wertheim, Helen
Williams, Scottie
Wilson, Dana

Index

Mail Order

Imagine the flavors of New Mexico delivered right to your doorstep!
Bueno Foods now offers frozen green and red chile, jarred ready-to-serve
chile sauces and salsas, dried chile powders, dry posole, blue cornmeal
and other Southwestern specialty items. Gift packs too!

Item No.	Item Description
3902-0	Green Chile Hot 6–13 oz.
3903-0	Green Chile Mild 6–13 oz.
3915-0	Green Chile Hot 3–13 oz./Green Chile Mild 3–13 oz.
3904-0	Red Chile Hot 6–14 oz.
3906-0	Green Chile Hot 3–13 oz./Red Chile Hot 3–14 oz.
3907-0	Green Chile Mild 3–13 oz./Red Chile Mild 3–14 oz.
3910-0	Premium Chimayó Chile Powder 4–12 oz.
3911-0	New Mexico Chile Powder Hot 8–6 oz.
3912-0	New Mexico Chile Powder Mild 8–6 oz.
3913-0	Dry Posole 4–12 oz.
3914-0	Blue Cornmeal 4–12 oz.
0126-1	Grandma's Flour Tortillas 12–1 dz. packages
3922-0	Chile Pantry 3–16 oz. ea. Hot, Salsa/Red Sauce/Green Sauce
3923-0	Taste of New Mexico Gift Box
3924-0	Sauce Sizzler 3–16 oz. ea Hot, Green Chile Sauce
3937-0	Children's Picture Book—Benito's Bizcochitos
3901-2	Cookbook—The Seasons: A Cookbook For Life

For over 50 years, our full product line is also available in grocery stores across New Mexico.

Bueno Foods
P.O. Box 293
Albuquerque, New Mexico 87103
www.buenofoods.com
1-800-95CHILE

A Taste of Enchantment

The Junior League of Albuquerque
P.O. Box 8858
Albuquerque, New Mexico 87198-8858
(505) 260-0199   (800) 753-7731
Fax: (505) 260-0393   E-mail: info@jlabq.org

YOUR ORDER	QUANTITY	TOTAL
A Taste of Enchantment @ $22.95 per book		$

Simply Simpatico @ $16.95 per book
   The Home of Authentic Southwestern Cuisine
   ** Tabasco® Hall of Fame Winner **
		$

Shipping and Handling $4.00 per book; $1.50 each additional copy		$
Total		$

Name

Street Address

City   State   Zip

Telephone

[   ] Check enclosed payable to the Junior League of Albuquerque
[   ] Charge to: [   ] Visa   [   ] MasterCard

Account Number

Cardholder Name

Signature

Photocopies will be accepted.

now we're cooking